"HURRY-SICKNESS"

People who handle stress badly tend to be nervous, irritable, impatient. They may suffer from aches and pains. They may have trouble sleeping. They may feel depressed and angry.

They are the victims of "hurry sickness," an affliction as prevalent as the common cold, and, left untreated, as potentially dangerous as cancer.

Women are now prey to stress as never before. Whether you are a homemaker, a career woman, a student, or all three, you owe it to yourself to find out how well you are handling the stress in your life. If you find through the tests and questionnaires in this book that you are a victim of stress, it's time to clarify your values, clean up your anxious mental habits, and make stress work for you rather than against you.

Stress can be the spice of life or the doorway to despair. With this book as your guide, you can make that choice.

MORE TEMPESTUOUS ROMANCES!

GOLDEN TORMENT (1323, $3.75)
by Janelle Taylor
Kathryn had travelled the Alaskan wilderness in search of her father. But after one night of sensual pleasure with the fierce, aggressive lumberjack, Landis Jurrell—she knew she'd never again travel alone!

LOVE ME WITH FURY (1248, $3.75)
by Janelle Taylor
When Alexandria discovered the dark-haired stranger who watched her swim, she was outraged by his intrusion. But when she felt his tingling caresses and tasted his intoxicating kisses, she could no longer resist drowning in the waves of sweet sensuality.

BELOVED SCOUNDREL (1259, $3.75)
by Penelope Neri
Denying what her body admitted, Christianne vowed to take revenge against the arrogant seaman who'd tormented her with his passionate caresses. Even if it meant never again savoring his exquisite kisses, she vowed to get even with her one and only BELOVED SCOUNDREL!

PASSION'S GLORY (1227, $3.50)
by Anne Moore
Each time Nicole looked into Kane's piercing dark eyes, she remembered his cold-hearted reputation and prayed that he wouldn't betray her love. She wanted faithfulness, love and forever—but all he could give her was a moment of PASSION'S GLORY.

Available wherever paperbacks are sold, or order direct from the Publisher. Send cover price plus 50¢ per copy for mailing and handling to Zebra Books, 475 Park Avenue South, New York, N.Y. 10016. DO NOT SEND CASH.

THE WOMAN'S GUIDE TO ZERO STRESS

BY DAWN SOVA

ZEBRA BOOKS
KENSINGTON PUBLISHING CORP.

ZEBRA BOOKS

are published by

Kensington Publishing Corp.
475 Park Avenue South
New York, N.Y. 10016

Copyright © 1984 by Dawn Sova

All rights reserved. No part of this book may be reproduced in any form or by any means without the prior written consent of the Publisher, excepting brief quotes used in reviews.

First printing: May, 1984

Printed in the United States of America

To my little guy, Robby Gregor

CONTENTS

INTRODUCTION..............................9
1. STRESS AND THE
    AMERICAN WOMAN 15
   What is Stress? 16
   Who Are the Stressed? 17
   Why Are We Stressed? 19
2. THE FEMALE STRESS RESPONSE 29
   Reacting to Stress 30
   How Stress Affects Your Body...............38
   How Stress Affects You
       Psychologically 41
   Some Assistance in Dealing
       With Stress 44
3. WOMEN, STRESS AND ILLNESS.........47
   Stress and Disease........................48
   Pre-menstrual Syndrome...................54
   Anorexia Nervosa........................57
4. YOUR PERSONAL STRESSORS..........61
   Identifying Your Stressors 62
   Computing Your Stress Load 67
   Stress Personality Pattern
       Evaluation (SPPE) 75
5. NEGATIVE COPING TECHNIQUES 81
6. SO THIS IS YOUR LIFE! 101
   Clarifying Your Values....................107

    Development of a Secure
       Self-Image..........................110
    Good Mental Health Habits 111
    Nutrition and Exercise 114
    Learn to Relax 118
7. DEALING WITH THE INEVITABLES 135

THE MASTERING STRESS PROGRAM

8. WEEK ONE: GETTING
    TO KNOW YOU 155
9. WEEK TWO: LEARNING TO COPE......181
10. WEEK THREE: LEARNING
     TO MANAGE STRESS 199
11. WEEK FOUR: MAKING STRESS
     WORK FOR YOU 211
12. SOME FURTHER WORDS
     ON RELAXING 237

Introduction

Stress, burnout and overcommitment are terms which have invaded contemporary conversation. Until recently, such terms were largely a part of the male experience and were applied in describing the high-powered individuals who ran the nation's corporations, ministered to the nation's ills, and directed the nation's industries. The influx of women into key positions of responsibility in these areas has not only modified the male experience and upset the balance of power but it has also had a profound influence on women's lives.

While it is true that women are now assuming greater responsibility than they ever have in the professions, government and business, it is also true that they are faced with greater personal and professional pressures. Much has been written about the many roles which women are currently required to fill. The Superwoman must be a career professional, as well as a wife, mother, lover, nurturer, housekeeper, chauffeur, and whatever else her personal life demands. Unlike her male counterparts who may identify themselves with their professions, leaving the personal responsibilities to their wives or to the mothers of their children, the contemporary woman feels pressed to strive for perfection on all fronts. Faced with her many obligations, the Superwoman often wears herself out both physically and psychologically in trying to prove herself competent.

For the woman who chooses to pursue a career, marriage and motherhood, the strain of juggling roles becomes one of allotting enough time to each of these roles. Often, the day just doesn't have enough hours. A full day in a demanding job leaves little psychic or physical energy for taking on the duties which marriage and motherhood demand. After dealing with clients, supervisors, subordinates and the public, it is a rare woman who can cheerfully stride into her home to make preparations for dinner and the evening. Her children clamor for attention, her husband wants a sympathetic ear, the laundry needs to be done, the house must be cleaned, and Superwoman is expected to fill all these needs. In the rush to fulfill all of her perceived obligations, the contemporary woman often finds that her own needs go unmet. Even for the relatively rare woman who can afford full-time housekeepers, the many emotional claims on a woman's energy can be draining.

The situation is even more difficult for the single mother who is often the sole support of her family. Rising divorce rates have made the single-mother-headed family a common living arrangement. In addition to shouldering the major emotional responsibility for their families, single mothers also usually bear the major economic burden. Only one-third of single mothers receive regular support from their former spouses. For the remaining two-thirds, financial support is either inadequate, sporadic, or nonexistent. Thus, already overburdened emotionally by the upheaval of divorce, the single mother is also financially overburdened. In addition, she must deal with the opinions of experts which place responsibility on the single mother for her children's every personality inadequacy.

Whether a married or single parent, the Superwoman is permitted little time for socializing or for enjoying personal pleasures. While theirs may be the more difficult situations, it is not only the Superwomen who are stressed but most women in modern society. Still a minority in positions of power, women are strenuously tested in ways that become unthinkable if applied to a male. In essence, whatever her approach to the job, a woman can expect criticism from some quarter. If she functions as a strong and assertive manager, a woman is condemned as pushy while her male counterpart is commended for being strong. The less assertive woman, on the other hand, runs the risk of being viewed as weak, ineffective and incompetent.

Even the woman who chooses to stay out of the work force may become a victim of the stress that is created by nagging doubts as to whether or not she is fulfilling her roles adequately. Should she be working and competing like her sisters? Is she a stimulating companion for her mate? Are her children receiving the best mothering possible? The list goes on and on.

INTRODUCTION

The societal pressures to which women are vulnerable are further complicated by the unique biologic pressures that women experience. Many of us who compete daily in the formerly all-male dominions would like to deny it, but our bodies do follow a calendar. While hormones cannot be used as an excuse any longer for keeping women out of high-paying jobs or challenging occupations, the issue of pre-menstrual syndrome has become scientific fact for large numbers of women. Studies have shown that cyclic, bodily changes make women more vulnerable than men to tension, and evidence has emerged to support the role of pre-menstrual syndrome in varying levels of mental disturbance. An extreme finding is that over eighty percent of all violent crimes committed by women have been found to occur in either the week preceding or during the woman's menstrual period.

The physical and psychological damage which results from stress are basically similar in both sexes. The sources and manifestations of stress, however, are unique to each sex. We must come to terms with the fact that being a woman demands wearing many hats, and being a woman demands that we fulfill our many roles competently. All of us face situations which make us grind our teeth, clench our fists, and long for release. The key to dealing successfully with such situations is not in avoiding them but in attacking our stressors head-on.

In the pages that follow, you will learn to identify the specific stressors in your life and the effects which they have on your body. As you follow the program, you will learn more about your own responses to such stressors and the ways in which you can modify these responses to prevent the physical and psychological damage which they wreak. You will learn to control stress by developing your own method of coping with your specific stressors. In short, you will learn to make stress work for you.

Let's begin.

1. Stress and the American Woman

Stress. The word conjures up tightened throats, clenched fists, grinding teeth and tense bodies. Your heart races madly while the blood pounds through your veins. Muscles constrict. You feel as if you are about to explode.

Perhaps your stress reaction is less dramatic. Your diaphragm tightens, making breathing difficult. Nervous perspiration soaks your clothing. Your head throbs with yet another nervous headache. Your stomach feels knotted and uncomfortable.

Whatever your response, if stress causes you

discomfort then you need to take control and make stress work for you.

WHAT IS STRESS?

Contrary to popular opinion and belief, stress is not nervous tension, nor is it the emergency discharge of adrenalin. It is not the same as an alarm reaction. Stress is, rather, any force, demand or pressure that requires a person to make an adjustment. It may be physical or psychological in origin.

Stress may emerge from physical activity or from mental/emotional activity. It doesn't matter if the situation is pleasant or unpleasant for stress to be present. What matters is the intensity of the demand that it places upon you to readjust.

For this reason, sad events such as the loss of a loved one, divorce, unwanted pregnancy, and losing a job are stress-producing. But happy events such as having a long-awaited baby, going to a big party, and marriage can be equally stressing. Regardless of the source of stress, the reaction of the body is relatively similar. Incidents, sad or happy, which cause stress are called stressors.

Stress is not always bad for us. Many

women actually thrive on stress because it makes their lives more challenging. As you may have guessed, the term stress is meaningful only when we apply it to a specific individual. What may offer a stimulating challenge to one woman might provide near-fatal stress to another. For the American woman, the range of stressors is vast. Stress emerges largely from the many roles which we are forced to play in going about our everyday lives.

WHO ARE THE STRESSED?

The image of the American woman, both projected and real, has undergone a major metamorphosis in past decades. New female roles have emerged and the traditional distinctions between the sexes have become blurred. Pop advertising proclaims, "You've come a long way, baby" while industries vie eagerly for the disposable income possessed by the growing number of women, both single and married, who have entered the employment market. The new Superwoman is offered a hair spray "that works as hard as you do," an eight-hour perfume "for the twenty-four-hour woman," and a variety of other products which perpetuate the myth of the working woman who can cook, clean, send the kids off to school, work a nine-to-five day, and still have enough time, energy and enthusiasm to let down her hair and seduce her favorite man in the evening after she does the dinner dishes.

While it is true that the image of women as either homemakers or career women devoid of homemaking responsibilities, but not as a blend of both, is rapidly becoming a view of the past as life styles change and new family configurations are sought, such media-perpetuated expectations continue. The structure of the so-called traditional family has undergone substantial change in the past few decades, bringing about an accompanying change in the needs and roles of the American woman. No longer bound to the home by repeated pregnancy or held back through a lack of educational opportunities as were our foremothers, we enjoy mobility and occupy a major place in the nation's economy. We are simultaneously filling the traditional roles and carving out new roles for ourselves as professionals, activists, consumers and individuals.

Now women face new conflicts which threaten to offset the professional progress that has been made. Stress and stress-related health problems have been identified as resulting from the all-too-common attempt to live up to the legend of the Superwoman who can deal successfully with the many demands placed on her by her personal and professional life. Indecision regarding marriage and childbearing, concern over what constitutes the appropriate feminine image in the competitive work world, and the difficulty of relationships with men, both personal and professional, result in a sense of inner turmoil over the conflicting desires and needs. Even in male-female relationships which espouse sharing, conflicts abound as society bombards the participants with messages of mixed approval. The conflict is often between our basic needs and desires and the expectations of others who fail to view women in anything but the most traditional light, however outmoded and irrelevant it may be for the contemporary scene. Thus, the expansion of our roles has also created a fertile breeding ground for new and more serious personal conflicts.

WHY ARE WE STRESSED?

Having less time and energy to carry on traditional roles of nurturing and housekeeping places extreme strain on women who still do not receive the social supports which men have long enjoyed. Conflicts and, thus, stressors emerge from decisions which we make regarding choice and the priority of values in the complex structure of our role(s). Such interior friction, or role conflict, may be integral to our existence as contemporary women but it also serves as a great source of stress, testing our coping abilities to the maximum.

That so many women do succeed in their many roles points to a greater ability to cope in women than in men. Our psychological makeup appears to be essentially responsible for our ability to fulfill the demands of whatever role we play, and points to a predisposition to play woman's role — or any other role. What is needed, however, is the acquisition of more effective skills to cope with the stressors which such demands create, skills which will permit us to master stress.

For many of us, neither our upbringing nor our early socialization prepares us to deal effectively with the stress of being a woman in contemporary society. Brought up to be non-competitive, nurturant, warm, gentle and non-aggressive, we often enter the workplace with difficulty, unaccustomed to exhibiting that which have been termed the masculine characteristics: being analytical, dominant, aggressive and competitive. The image of femininity, ingrained in us from early girlhood, has become blurred as more and more women enter the professional arena. Unfortunately, many women are seduced by the lure of power and tend to value the so-called masculine characteristics associated with success more than those characteristics which are a part of our early socialization. This creates a dilemma: We value both the male work role and the characteristics needed for success yet do not feel ourselves fully in possession of such traits.

Those women who do succeed in establishing a professional niche often come under fire for the very traits that typify hard work and dedication in the male.

On the other hand, the woman who chooses to remain a full-time homemaker and to refrain from entering the work world is also subject to stress as she watches others achieve. She must frequently deal with the question, "What do you do?" This contradiction persists in a society in which child-rearing customs continue to foster aggression and self-reliance in males and dependence in females. In spite of the rapid growth of industry and a constantly changing society, vestiges of old stereotypes remain in the United States. They are visible in the conflicting expectations about female life styles, the perception of men and women which most people retain, and in the relationship between the sexes.

Asked to apply specific adjectives to each gender, college students in one sex role study described women as being primarily affectionate, loyal, gentle, sympathetic and warm. Men were viewed as being analytical, ambitious, aggressive, independent and dominant.

In similar studies, individuals asked to provide word associations to "woman" provided adjectives and synonyms which fell into the following categories: housewife, bunny (sex object), clubwoman, career woman, and woman athlete. When respondents were further asked to create clusters of the words, the conceptualization of women emerged as either maternal figure/housewife, sex object/ bunny, or clubwoman/career woman/woman athlete. Both male and female respondents viewed the housewife and bunny as being incompatible, but only men expressed the feeling that the housewife and the independent woman (clubwoman/career woman/woman athlete) are devoid of similarity. Women attribute many characteristics to both, suggesting that women see two or more roles as compatible, if not vital, in one person. Men continue to view these roles as mutually exclusive.

With such strongly voiced and deeply ingrained views as to how contemporary women should act—either through custom or through presumed basic nature—there exists little question as to the *why* underlying the conflicts we suffer and the stressors that plague our lives.

While attitudes about traditional feminine and masculine traits may be slowly changing, women (both professional and the homemaker) remain trapped between the old and the new views, belonging fully to neither. Much attention has been focused on the working wife and mother with little note being given to the changing needs and concepts of the women who chooses to remain a full-time housewife. Generally viewed as an unproductive member of an achievement-oriented society, the homemaker often retreats into thin excuses and alibis when confronted with the question "What do you do?" She should answer that she is a "domestic engineer" as some wags have suggested, yet the fact remains that unpaid work is not valued in our society.

For most homemakers, the functions as well as the goals within the home have changed substantially due to the increasingly convenient and time-saving shopping facilities, services and products now available. Although the combination of nurturing and enrichment is absorbing and takes enormous amounts of time, energy, enthusiasm and imagination, there remains a negative attitude toward the homemaker. Placed in a role which, in theory, demands constant attendance to the emotional as well as the physical needs of others, the housewife can hardly be faulted for becoming bored, lonely and frustrated. As an added source of frustration, society tells her that her role is meaningless and unproductive as it simultaneously applauds her for being a traditional woman. Caught in this double bind, the homemaker can readily identify with the many women who eagerly nodded in agreement with Betty Friedan's call to action in *The Feminine Mystique*.

The position of the professional woman—married, divorced or never married—is equally confused by stereotypes which create substantial professional as well as personal stress. The unattractive, aggressive woman who possesses a quantity of those characteristics that are normally labelled masculine may find that her male co-workers and those female co-workers who prefer to use mere feminine wiles to advance professionally view her as a threat. Rather than be viewed as ambitious and competent, she may be ungraciously referred to as a "bitch" or "dyke."

Being attractive, on the other hand, is no better in most instances. Attractive women, however intelligent and talented, fall prey to being misunderstood by male colleagues, who view friendliness and warmth as efforts at seduction, and by less attractive female co-workers, in whom they stimulate jealousy. The attractive professional woman frequently finds herself viewed as a stereotypical bunny rather than as a competent professional.

Another disturbing source of stress in women, identified by psychologists in recent years, is the fear of success — success anxiety or success avoidance. The foundation of this conflict is open to debate. Some psychologists contend that men fundamentally have a stronger motive to achieve than do women. Others argue that women are actually afraid to succeed and, thus, attempt consciously and subconsciously to sabotage their own efforts. Such debate has led psychologists to question whether women actually have the personal characteristics necessary to a successful career, or if there remains an inherent contradiction between having a career and being feminine. To the many women who have competed successfully in formerly all-male professions, the question is asinine. To those who feel inadequate, uncertain and insecure, however, the question serves as one more source of stress.

The stressors produced by the fear of success, and by competing against substantial odds, are severe. Although studies show that many anxious women are successful despite their anxiety, a high price is exacted. Not only do they contend with psychosomatic ailments such as headaches, ulcers, colitis and insomnia, and a host of other more serious illnesses, but they also face feelings of ambivalence about themselves and their relationships with others.

The toll taken in human lives by such stress is tragic. Statistics show that the suicide rate among women has risen dramatically in recent decades as greater numbers of women have entered the labor force. The suicide rate for female doctors and female medical students is four times the rate of that for women in general in the United States. Female psychologists have a suicide rate three times greater than the general female population. Further, even though less than two percent of the American Chemical Society membership is female, the ACS reports that women make up eleven percent of the suicides among its members.

One can place the blame on the same professional pressures or health-related problems that affect the male population. However, the fact that the majority of such suicides occur among young, healthy and successful women points to other factors. Although greater numbers of women are confidently establishing careers first and then turning their thoughts to marriage and raising a family, societal and cultural pressures still exist. It is only in the last decade that young career women have had the security of role models to emulate. Their professional ancestors were isolated by their small numbers and by the need to compete alone in professions which had formerly been impenetrable to women. Frustration and depression, rather than networking and meaningful professional relationships, have for too long been the lot of the career woman.

In essence, the key to combatting the stress experienced by women in the workplace lies in a reordering of society's view of the roles that men and women play. Such massive change requires extensive and revolutionary organized action. There has been a movement in this direction for the last two decades. But whatever the strides that have been made, each of us must learn to cope effectively with our present situation. This means that the stressors that bombard us daily must be individually confronted, controlled and mastered.

Because of the extensive damage which stressors can inflict on both your body and your mind, learning to master stress is vital. To successfully combat stress, you must first identify both the source of stress in your life and your responses (both negative and positive) to these stressors. In the chapters that follow, you will learn more about your stressors and your specific stress responses. As you follow the four-week program, you will develop a method of coping and of taking control of your life.

2. The Female Stress Response

Few women are fully aware of the numerous stressors that bombard them daily. As a result, they tend to view their responses to these stressors merely as bad habits. Nervous twitches, twirling hair, scratching nonexistent itches, and gulping down large quantities of coffee are, of course, bad habits. They are also the actions which many women exhibit when the going gets rough.

Few of us consciously relate the severe stomach cramps which may occur in mid-menstrual cycle with stress, yet this is one response. Many of us point to upper respiratory infections and the virus which appears to linger for months at a time as being the result of germs in the air, but these too result from increased susceptibility due to stress. Further, how many women are aware that their difficult days with children, husbands, lovers and others around them are the result of stressors in other areas acting upon them?

To a great extent, we respond to our stressors in a habitual manner, usually without the least awareness of the implications of the response.

REACTING TO STRESS

As many researchers have pointed out, our modern reactions to stress have their roots in the reactions of our primitive ancestors to physical dangers. The fight-or-flight impulse, which can still be commonly observed among street criminals as well as in the animal world, was an emergency reaction which allowed our ancestors to fight harder and run faster than the source of their stress. Hardly cerebral, the emergency reactions of our ancestors helped them to survive in an environment which presented them with actual physical dangers. Electrical and chemical messages were sent from the brain to various parts of their bodies, signaling the muscles to either fight or to flee.

Chemical messengers, which began in the part of the brain called the hypothalamus, signaled the pituitary glands which, in turn, activated the adrenal glands. These adrenal glands released special hormones into the blood stream of our ancestors which helped them survive.

Physiologically, the electrical and chemical messages created that which today we recognize as our own reactions to stress. For primitive humans, muscles became tense so that they could move faster and fight harder. Their hearts speeded up to pump more blood and to deliver greater amounts of energy and oxygen. The stressed individual breathed harder, allowing the body to take in more oxygen and rid itself of carbon dioxide. The digestive process slowed down or stopped completely. Contraction of blood vessels at the skin level allowed blood to go to the parts of the body needed for fighting—the large muscles, the heart and the lungs. In addition, the muscles that controlled the bowels and bladder were relaxed in order that excess weight, by way of waste, could be released.

At this point, you may be questioning how this primitive stress reaction relates to the contemporary woman burdened with more psychological than physical stressors. In theory, our reactions to threatening situations, either positive or negative, are handled in a nonphysical and so-called civilized manner. Although the animal in the forest can still operate under a fight-or-flight system, making spontaneous decisions in reaction to a threat, most humans sublimate such reactions. We cannot physically strike out at the source of our stressors, nor can we turn tail and run from them. Instead, we have developed a set of emotional and psychological responses to stress.

For many women, frequent bombardment by stressors in the home, at work, and in society produces a condition of near-perpetual stress in which the fight-or-flight stress response becomes an ingrained behavioral pattern. As stressors build up, the stress reactions build up. We are constantly bombarded by stimuli which cause fight-or-flight reactions that we no longer even recognize as stress responses. A perpetually engaged fight-or-flight mechanism results in a state of deadened awareness.

Before you test your own reactions to a specific stressor which has physical implications, think about the implications of a perpetually engaged fight-or-flight mechanism. Think about those women whom you have heard described as being "nervous as a race horse" or who frequently say that they have no patience with fools. What about the woman who sits on the edge of her seat as she waits for an appointment, then bristles when she is told that the doctor or other professional is several minutes late? Have you watched some mothers of young children in the supermarket, always reaching out and grabbing items out of the reach of their offspring *before* the child has even thought about extending a hand? What about the woman with the high-pitched, loud laugh, or the one who giggles most of the time? The nail-biter? The constant talker? The woman who always appears to be on the move? These are women who are in states of near-constant stress response. They are hardly pleasant company either to themselves or to those around them.

Are you aware of your own stress responses? In order to examine the manner in which you respond to stress at the most basic level, that of the physical, try this imaging exercise.

EXERCISE-IMAGING

For a moment, stop and examine this fight-or-flight reaction and its meaning for you now, in contemporary society. Sit back in a comfortable chair and allow your body to relax and become loose. Now, imagine that it is a warm spring or summer evening. The air is sweet-smelling. There is a cool breeze blowing softly against your skin. You are out for a walk down a familiar street in a familiar neighborhood. You are peacefully walking along alone, letting your mind roam tranquilly. *Allow your mind to build up an image of serenity.* There is no one around and you are glad to have the solitude.

You walk along for a few minutes, enjoying yourself, lulled into complacency. Suddenly you hear the sound of footsteps behind you. You look around but see no one—only the quivering of bushes off the walk behind you. You walk on and hear the sound of twigs being trampled on. You walk faster. The sounds come faster and appear to be closer.

Allow your body to react as if this were really happening to you. Experience, for the moment, the fear or apprehension of being alone on a deserted street, formerly friendly but now menacing. What is your emergency reaction? Identify your response in a fight-or-flight situation. Did your throat tighten? Did your heart begin to beat harder? Did your body tense? Did your legs tense? Your arms? Your neck? Did flutters appear in your stomach? Write your responses on the lines below.

_____

_____

_____

_____

_____ .

The artificiality of the situation may at first inhibit your fully imagining the scene to the point that an actual physical response emerges. Try it a few times and note your increasingly acute responses. Each time you repeat the imaging exercise, you should become aware of additional physical or psychological reactions which are part of the larger fight-or-flight response. Is your response primarily physical? Psychological? What do you feel that this says about your personality and your experience with stressors?

The imaging exercise may seem difficult if you have never been in a similar situation. Most women, however, can recall at least one instance in which they felt themselves physically threatened. Certainly, the likelihood of physical danger is very real to all women in the United States, considering that the annual incidence of rape is one in every 3000 women, that spouse abuse is all too common, and that all manner of violent crime has increased in the last decade. Even if you are fortunate enough never to have experienced the threat of someone stalking you, gauging your reactions in such a situation can be enlightening, preparing you to clear-headedly and reasonably confront this stressful incident if it ever happens to you.

An easier exercise for many women is recalling a specific stressful incident that happened recently.

EXERCISE-RECALL

Relax your mind and body for a moment by sitting back in a chair. Close your eyes if you wish. Now, search your memory for a recent time in which you felt stressed in an everyday occurrence. Replay the scene in your mind, remembering how others who were present acted. Recall how upset you felt and the manner and the intensity in which you responded to the upset. What was your reaction?

Identify your reaction to stress in the real life situation and compare it to the reaction you had in imagining the physical danger of being stalked on a lonely and darkened street. Were you able to arouse the same amount of emotional response in both situations? How were the reactions similar? How were they different? Did your throat tighten? Did your heart begin to beat harder? Did your body tense? Did your legs tense? Your arms? Your neck? Did flutters appear in your stomach? Write your responses on the lines below.

_____

_____

_____

_____

_____ .

Now, assess your reactions in both situations. Did the real-life situation point out any specific ways in which you responded to the source of stress? Did you react with a full-fledged fight-or-flight response to the everyday stressor, even though physical danger was not present? Was this reaction characteristic of your response to other stress-filled situations?

If you geared up for action and made a decision either to fight or to flee in the stressful situation that you recalled, take comfort in the fact that you are not alone. Many women find that their stress reactions follow a well-defined pattern of adaptation to specific stresses of life. First we become upset in the situation, perhaps floundering in our attempts to extricate ourselves from the stressful situation. Then we react to the point that we overcome our stressors—or our systems break down and the stressors, in effect, overcome us. Although the pattern becomes psychologically and physically predictable, it, nonetheless, encourages a variety of serious physical and psychological ills.

HOW STRESS AFFECTS YOUR BODY

Stress is not basically bad for women. It is overstress that is harmful. Anyone who is ambitious or who has goals in life must learn to live with stress.

An often-used example of excessive stress is the comparison of the turtle and the race horse. If a turtle is forced to run like a race horse, it will die. You can't make a racehorse out of a turtle. Similarly, a race horse made to act like a turtle suffers from stress since his basic biologic nature is forced to change. Place yourself in the body of either animal. Which one are you?

Most of us could name women we know who fit into one or the other of these two categories — women who find fulfillment in their limited role but are extremely stressed when required to expand their roles. A good example of this is the so-called displaced homemaker whose case has been advanced in recent years.

The classic displaced homemaker is a woman in her late forties or early fifties whose twenty years or more of married life have been spent in being a homemaker. The role has kept her so busy that she never found the time to acquire skills that would help her find a job. She defends herself by pointing out that she did not have the time, that mothering, caring for her husband, and homemaking provided more than full-time employment. When her husband announces that he is leaving the marriage, the displaced homemaker is forced to give up her role as homemaker for a life in which she must earn a living. As the former turtle become a race horse, the period of transition can provide numerous stressors.

Similarly, the woman who juggles motherhood, career, recreational activities, marriage, and other involvements may find that the lack of time is occasionally stressful but that the pace is exhilarating. Suppose that this woman loses her job, or that she becomes ill and must spend time quietly recuperating. What do you think this change of pace, from the breathless whirl to a tortoiselike crawl, will do to her? The race horse is forced to change its nature drastically, if only temporarily, and the strain of chomping at the bit while waiting to resume activity will prove extremely stressful.

Aside from the physical damage which stress causes, there are a variety of psychological ramifications.

HOW STRESS AFFECTS YOU PSYCHOLOGICALLY

Even before the physical element enters the picture, stress begins to effect psychological damage. Even worse than the physiological reaction, stress has an identifiable bad effect on a person's psychological and emotional well-being.

Stressed individuals suffer from depression, chronic anxiety, guilt, hostility and shame. Some act out in decidedly anti-social ways such as alcoholism, child and spouse abuse, and even incest. Excessive stress makes an individual emotionally sick. The internal and external controls break down.

Perhaps more than men, women's lives are profoundly touched by the negative stress responses of alcoholism and child abuse. Male alcohol abusers have customarily been a more visible group and, thus, the treatment opportunities and success rates have naturally been better for men than for women. Alcoholism rates among women have been rising in the past decade but this change is probably not so much due to increased drinking as it is to a greater exposure of the alcohol problem among women. In the past, homemakers who responded to stress by drinking could hide their problem behind darkened windows. The female executive, due to the rarity of the problem, would strive to keep her drinking problem out of the office. She already has one major handicap in being female. A drinking problem that might be viewed sympathetically in a male could spell professional suicide for a woman.

The low visibility of the female problem drinker meant that little treatment was being offered to these women, and few statistics were available regarding the extent of the problem. Today, a greater awareness of alcohol abuse as a disease has emerged and greater numbers of women are entering treatment. But there are still large numbers whose daily stress drive them to the bottle — and greater frustration in their lives.

A similar problem exists regarding the abuse of such prescription drugs as Valium and Librium which helps to tranquilize the stressed. Although legal, these drugs are frequently mixed with alcohol to further dull the pain of stress. They are a dangerous response to the problem.

Another serious psychological response to stress is reflected by the high rate of child abuse in this nation. It is not surprising that the greater number of child abusers are women because women still do the majority of parenting. Frustrated by their economic burdens and unable to deal with the stress that inadequate housing, conflicting roles and intense emotional responsibility have placed upon them, women may find themselves acting irrationally. While they may love their children very much, these children are the most available outlet for their pent-up emotions. Uncontrolled rage and frustration become life-threatening stressors which can cause permanent damage within the family and to those we love.

In addition, a psychological reaction to stress festers and stimulates life-threatening physiological responses, such as heart disease and other ailments. The psychological effect of stress can also effectively destroy your love life, as any of you who have found yourselves with clammy palms, a rigid body, and a lack of desire due to fear can attest. Certainly, even if the threat of physical devastation hasn't convinced you that it's time to confront your stressors and to learn to master them, the threat to your love life should spur you on to action.

This litany of ills is not meant to frighten

you or make you curtail your life's activities. Instead, it is intended to point out the severity of the problem of stress and to encourage you to take stock in both the stressors in your life and of your responses to stress. Stress is beneficial to most of us, it adds spice to what would be a dull existence. However, as with any spice, stress must be used sparingly. Too much stress destroys the very entity which it is meant to enhance. Too little stress is futile since it adds nothing.

The Mastering Stress Program is designed to aid you in developing the right mix of stress in your own life, tempered by your particular needs. Although several more sophisticated techniques for coping with your stressors appear in the program, the following brief exercise is helpful in relieving some of the tension which stress can create.

SOME ASSISTANCE IN DEALING WITH STRESS

Sit back in a comfortable chair; place both feet on the ground. Breathe in deeply through your nose, keeping your mouth closed. Then exhale deeply through your mouth, emptying your lungs totally. Breathe in deeply through your nose once again with your mouth closed. Exhale deeply through your mouth, emptying your lungs totally. Do this breathing exercise five times. Feel the tension leave your body as you force all of the air out of your lungs.

When stress makes you tense, try this breathing technique as a temporary means of alleviating some of the strain.

3. Women, Stress and Illness

Not only is excessive stress psychologically upsetting, it can shorten life by increasing the risk of cardiovascular disease, ulcers and the incidence of high blood pressure, by inducing swollen joints, stomach and muscle problems, and by lowering resistance to respiratory infection. Women who are stress-prone frequently suffer from headaches, muscle aches, cold and sweaty hands, and a variety of other mysterious and equally disturbing ailments.

Laboratory experiments conducted by Hans Selye, the major authority in the field of stress research, have shown that stress is a factor in the following ailments:

1. High blood pressure
2. Heart disease
3. Blood vessel disorders
4. Diseases of the kidney
5. Convulsions
6. Rheumatic and rheumatoid arthritis
7. Inflammatory diseases of the skin and the eyes
8. Infections
9. Allergies
10. Nervous and mental disease
11. Sexual derangements
12. Sexual dysfunction
13. Digestive disease
14. Metabolic disease
15. Cancer

Although not all scientists are convinced that stress syndrome plays a major role in all of these afflictions, most at least admit that it has a substantial effect on high blood pressure and heart disease.

STRESS AND DISEASE

The connection between disease and stress is of special interest to women because the formerly wide gender gap in the number of deaths from cardiovascular disease, high blood pressure, cancer and other major illness has been decreasing yearly. Half of all deaths in the United States are linked to heart disease and ten percent of American adults have a peptic ulcer. Each year, one hundred thousand new cases of breast cancer are reported and rates of incidence for other cancers are also increasing.

Physicians have also reported an increase in such psychosomatic illness as pre-menstrual tension and anorexia nervosa as a health-care and treatment problem. The U.S. Health Center has reported that five billion doses of tranquilizers, three billion doses of amphetamines, and five billion doses of barbiturates are prescribed yearly. Such statistics do not include non-prescription and illegal drugs. Of the prescriptions, most are willing to provide medication to alleviate the primary symptoms of stress—fatigue, hypertension and insomnia.

Stress-related disease has increased to the point where doctors have identified stress as our number one health problem.

Let's take a look at some sobering statistics. Nearly one million Americans die each year from cardiovascular disease. Although such factors as obesity, high levels of cholesterol, hypertension, inactivity, heredity, and cigarette smoking have long been associated with heart disease, there now exists considerable evidence of a direct relationship between stress and heart disease. Researchers have demonstrated that heart accidents can be induced chemically in laboratory animals by increasing stress levels even without closing off the arteries of the heart. Forced exercise, frustration—almost any kind of stressor has been shown to have the potential to cause death by cardiac failure.

In addition, numerous cases of sudden deaths brought on by psychological stress have been documented. Among these are the impact of death, severe grief, the threat of loss of a friend or mate, the loss of self-esteem or status, or the threat of injury. Sudden deaths linked to stress have also been observed when a danger has passed, or even during a reunion, triumph or happy ending.

Cardiologists Meyer Friedman and Ray Rosenman have studied people's habits and personalities of people to determine which individuals are most susceptible to heart disease. They have found that those who are aggressive, hostile, competitive and easily provoked — whom they identify as Type A — are the most common victims of cardiac problems. In these individuals, a propensity to stressful behavior combined with high-powered life styles provides the foundation for their cardiac problems.

A similarly strong link exists between hypertension or high blood pressure and stress. The Center for Disease Control estimates that between twenty three and forty four million Americans currently suffer from hypertension and that the disease is responsible for over sixty thousand deaths yearly. Although diet, heredity, race and obesity have been implicated as the cause of hypertension, stress is an equally strong contender. When the body encounters real or imagined threats, it responds instantly by increasing the blood pressure in order to rush an oversupply of blood to various areas of the body. If some unconscious stress remains after the immediate danger has passed, the pressure may remain high, thus creating long-term stress on the blood vessels.

Cancer has also been related to excessive stress. The American Cancer Society reports that the disease claims the lives of more than 750 thousand Americans yearly. The social stress theory of cancer has received increased support by scientific research in recent years. Dr. W.B. Gross, professor of veterinary medicine at the Virginia Polytechnic Institute, has studied stress in chickens and derived results which hold substantial relevance for humans. The pecking order of chickens represents a social hierarchy comparable to that in human society. To examine the effect of social stress on chickens, Dr. Gross and his fellow researchers compared cancer incidence between two groups of chickens, one in which the pecking was deliberately disrupted and one in which the pecking order remained intact. Chickens who experienced social stress were found to be eight times more likely to develop cancer than the group of chickens in which the pecking order remained intact.

In a study of 450 cancer patients at New York's Institute of Applied Biology over a twelve-year period, three psychological characteristics were found to appear more frequently in cancer patients than in persons not suffering from cancer: (1) The majority of them had experienced the loss of a very important personal relationship before identification of their disease; (2) Almost half of them appeared to vent feelings of hostility toward others; (3) Greater than one third of them showed significant levels of tension regarding the death of one of their parents, even if the death had occurred many years before.

Such linking of stress with cancer is being investigated even further today. While not the only factor, stress has been shown, certainly, to be an important factor.

An increased susceptibility to illness in general is one notable result of stress. Ulcers have long been accepted as emanating from a stressful existence. Gastric disturbance initiates ulceration of the stomach lining, and stress increases and perpetuates the amount of gastric disturbance.

A link between stress and diabetes has been uncovered in recent years and doctors have included warnings about stress in their treatment of diabetic patients. When a person is under stress, the blood sugar level rises. If the condition is permitted to continue for a long while, an excessive burden is placed on the pancreas so that it finally fails to produce enough insulin.

Backaches and headaches are among the more common manifestations of stress. Muscle tension, constricting of blood vessels, and migraine headaches are all due to excessive stress. In addition to the fact that a person is more susceptible to illness when highly stressed, a variety of other ailments have been linked to stress, such as allergies, arthritis, and sexual dysfunction.

Based on this brief review of the link between physical complaints and stress, you can see that stress is a serious health problem for everyone.

For women, however, there also exists the often debilitating pain of pre-menstrual syndrome, a combination of physical and psychological responses to our stressors.

PRE-MENSTRUAL SYNDROME (PMS)

The issue of pre-menstrual tension has achieved media prominence due to several legal disputes in which the condition has been used as a defense for women who have committed violent crimes. In two cases in Britain, women have walked free from the criminal courts after heated debate among doctors, lawyers and feminists as to whether mitigating circumstances created by PMS were grounds for acquittal in cases of murder and attempted murder. Similar pleas have been registered in U.S. courts.

Although the erratic behavior of generations of women has been lightly explained away by noting, "It's that time of the month," and doctors have been aware for over fifty years that pre-menstrual hormonal changes have significant effect on behavior, it is not until recently that serious attention has been paid to the problem. The issue of PMS poses a dual problem for women: It is exacerbated by the other stressors in a woman's life and is itself a source of stress.

As long ago as 1931, Dr. R.T. Frank published a scientific paper which described the condition as he had witnessed it among his patients. The common physical symptoms of PMS may include swelling of the abdomen, migraine headaches, a general feeling of bloatedness, breast soreness, pain in the back, skin disorders, small skin hemorrhages, and a stuffed nose, asthma or other respiratory disorder. Coupled with these physical symptoms, which may appear from two to fourteen days before the onset of the period, are the mental symptoms which are strongly related to stress. Sufferers are extremely tense, irritable, often depressed, lethargic and prone to feeling clumsy in everything they do. Their psychological state functions as a source of intense stress during the pre-menstrual period which, in turn, produces further stressors to exacerbate the symptoms.

The extent of susceptibility to PMS is hotly debated although consensus appears to be that at least forty percent of all women between fourteen and fifty suffer to some degree from PMS. For approximately ten to twelve percent of these women, the severity of the condition has a serious negative effect on their lives and they are involved in regular treatment. Studies have shown that the highest rate of medical treatment is requested by women who are in the pre-menstrual phase, and that from seventy nine to eighty four percent of all violent crimes committed by women occur at this time.

A link between pre-menstrual tension and stress has been supported by Hans Selye who pointed out nearly twenty years ago that one's ability to adapt is severely curtailed in the pre-menstrual phase. Physical changes such as water retention, various allergic and hypersensitive reactions, vascular seizures, and physical pain produce psychological responses which often appear to be meaningless and difficult to restrain.

The woman who suffers from pre-menstrual tension is stressed by the experience.

Her responses further increase her stress, thus producing more severe stressors. The deranged behavior which some women manifest, such as abnormal hunger, general emotional instability, and an increase in sexual drive, further complicates an already stressful situation.

Cravings for salt provide temporary solace, but result in greater water retention, swelling of tissues, alteration of the metabolism, and an increased bloated feeling. The PMS/stress cycle is vicious. As with any other stress-related condition, learning to control our stressors can also lead to a lessening of the damage which PMS can inflict upon us.

Another stress-related disorder that more commonly afflicts females than males is that of anorexia nervosa.

ANOREXIA NERVOSA

The condition of anorexia nervosa is the systematic starving to death of apparently physiologically healthy young women whose ages usually range from eleven to twenty five. While the condition is not limited to young women, only fifteen percent of the cases reported yearly have been identified in males.

A variety of theories have been advanced in the attempt to explain this phenomenon. Many clinicians and families of anorectics blame our thinness-obsessed culture. Societal pressure supposedly drives young women to extremes to obtain that look. More recently, however, researchers have determined that a variety of complex interpersonal relationships and self-concept inadequacies play important roles in encouraging the development of this psychosomatic syndrome.

The issues of power and powerlessness are integral to understanding the phenomenon. Instead of the earlier exclusive focus of clinicians on regression and oral drive components, they are now exploring various ego deficits and specific perceptual-conceptual deficits in the life of the anorectic. Clinicians assert that three main ego disturbances are responsible for anorexia nervosa: distortions of body image; perception; and sense of effectiveness in social dealings.

In essence, it is control, the desire for autonomy and effectiveness, that is the key to the condition.

The severity of the anorexia nervosa condition exhibited by a young woman has been found to be strongly related to the degree of control that she feels in her life. The woman who feels manipulated and powerless, who can see no way out of her powerless state, may attempt to control her other human needs by controlling the basic drive of hunger. The anorectic becomes involved in a ceaseless struggle to gain control over her body and her life. By starving herself, she gains a degree of self-determination in one small area in her life. The anorectic uses her condition to exert an element of control over her environment and, in essence, experiences a sense of freedom even while she destroys her body.

Because she cannot cope consciously with the pressures of powerlessness, the anorectic subconsciously wills herself to starve.

The symptoms of the condition must be handled on both a medical level, to increase weight gain, and on a psychological level. Learning to cope with the stressors which have precipitated the condition may be the most valuable approach to overcoming anorexia nervosa.

The range of illnesses which our stressors can stimulate is vast. Women who are stressed share with men a susceptibility to heart disease, hypertension, cancer, ulcers, diabetes, and physical pain. Our stress reactions, however, extend beyond these complaints. For many women, everyday stressors increase premenstrual tension and menstrual discomfort. In addition, stress can seriously jeopardize life in stimulating the development of anorexia nervosa, a condition which afflicts mainly women.

To successfully avoid the ravages to the body that stress can effect, you must become aware of your specific stressors.

4. Your Personal Stressors

The second chapter gave you the opportunity to assess your stress patterns through imagining and/or recalling a stress-filled situation. For many of you, this may have been the first time that you took the time to note not only *what* stimulates your stressors (the stimuli of your stress response) but *how* you respond, often unconsciously, to stress (the result of these stimuli). Before you can begin to learn to control stress, you must first be aware of your particular stressors and of the response which they elicit from you.

Once you are aware of the stressors in your life, and once you identify the manner in which you react to these stressors, you can begin to combat them. You can then formulate a method for mastering stress.

IDENTIFYING YOUR STRESSORS

It's time to create a profile of your individual stress load and of the patterns in your life which encourage stress. As more than one military strategist has determined, the first step in overcoming the enemy is getting to know him. In this case, not *stress* but *unmanaged stress* is your enemy. It must be overcome and controlled — but not eliminated from your life. Remember that no life is stress-free; the only complete freedom from stress is death. Some women thrive in a stress-filled existence. They find that stress makes life more exciting.

There are, however, differences between states of stress. Positive stress is often a short-term response to a stressor. Once the stressor is no longer present, body equilibrium returns and we relax for a time. Short-term stress is functional in moderate amounts. It provides the energy to complete an education, to strive for a promotion, and to reach creative peaks.

Long-term stress, on the other hand, is often counterproductive, at best. While moderate short-term stress is essential to life, long-term stress places a heavy strain on our bodies and emotions. As increasingly higher levels of prolonged and uninterrupted stress occur, the body remains "on edge." Women who suffer from such prolonged stress are often described by such adjectives as irritable, edgy, nervous, high-strung, indicating that they are doing a poor job of dealing with their sources of stress.

Over time, the base-line levels of activity of the body become permanently raised. For example, your normal heart rate may have been seventy beats per minute when you first reached adulthood, several years and many incidents later it may have risen to a normal (for you) eighty beats per minute. Blood pressure and other bodily functions that assist the body in returning to a normal steady state are similarly raised to new levels as a result of long-term stress. They are only normal in the sense that they now represent the consistent measure of your heart rate, pulse, or other function. The implications for your health are serious.

Each of us has a specific *stress threshold* which we can only identify after observing our experience with stressors and stress. What may be stressful to one woman might not necessarily trigger the stress reaction in the body or mind of another woman. Repeated experience with stressors can make an individual better able to tolerate them, and can aid in making them productive rather than destructive.

It is, in the final analysis, not the intensity of the stressor which wreaks havoc with our physical and psychological health. Nor is it the intensity that determines the extent of the reaction. Rather, the amount of damage which stress accomplishes is dependent upon how you react to a particular stressor.

You can compare the stress reaction to the experience of the movie stuntwoman. For most of us, a fall from the second story of a building, a leap through a blazing fire, or an auto crash at sixty miles per hour would probably signal our death. We don't know how to break a fall, nor do we have the expertise (or willingness) to leap through fire. And we don't, as a matter of course, have the necessary equipment and safeguards to avert death in a sixty-mph head-on collision. Yet, movie stuntwomen perform such stunts—and walk away unscathed. How do they do it? To the knowledgeable, it's simple. They are well-trained in the techniques necessary to escape injury, and they make certain that they have the proper equipment to keep from being injured.

The same holds true in coming to terms with stress. Identical stressors do not elicit identical reactions in different people. Someone caught unprepared (i.e., one who is not aware of the nature of her stressors or who does not know to deal effectively with stress) is likely to sustain more physiologic and emotional damage than the woman who knows the enemy.

Take a look at the variety of stressors which plagued you this past week. Make a list. What situations and people created stress for you in the past week? Spouse? Lover? Kids? In-laws? Work? Unpaid bills? Car? House? List as many as you can think of and then examine the sources of stress.

Although this list only reflects the incidents of one week, you will be surprised to find that quite a few stressors may be listed. Even more important, you will probably observe from your list that it is more often the little hassles of life rather than the major crises which plague you most.

Drs. Thomas H. Holmes and Richard C. Rahe, psychiatrists at the University of Washington Medical School, confirm that the routine problems of life have greater impact on individuals. Similarly, relief from stress is not necessarily found in dramatic good luck or in a sudden betterment of one's present life. Instead, a variety of common, everyday uplifts improve a woman's ability to cope effectively with her stressors. Thus, winning the lottery, although it has a lot of advantages, does less to help the individual cope with stress than such common realities as good health and adequate sleep.

Following are the ten most frequently reported sources of stress found by Holmes and Rahe, as well as the ten most frequently reported stress fighters.

LIFE'S COMMON STRESSORS

1. concern about weight
2. health of self or family member
3. rising prices of supermarket and common goods
4. care of the home — inside
5. lack of personal time
6. chronic forgetfulness
7. care of the home — outside
8. property ownership, investments, or taxes

9. rising crime rates
10. personal appearance

STRESS FIGHTERS

1. good relationship with spouse or lover
2. good relationship with friends
3. completion of desirable projects
4. good health
5. sleeping well
6. dining out
7. fulfilling obligations
8. making personal contact with others by phone or in person
9. having demand-free time with family
10. being satisfied with one's surroundings

As you can see, it is the little hassles of daily living that can be harmful as they accumulate.

It's time to evaluate your individual stress load and to determine your stress level.

COMPUTING YOUR STRESS LOAD

On the Compustress form which follows, place a check next to those events which have occurred in the last year and those situations which are characteristic of your behavior or experience in the past year. After you've finished, count the number of items checked and compare that number with the scores and explanations which follow the form.

COMPUSTRESS

Instructions: Check those events which have occurred in the last year and those situations which are characteristic of your behavior or experience in the past year.

____ 1. Experienced difficulty sleeping at night
____ 2. Felt nervous or restless
____ 3. Experienced a serious illness
____ 4. Someone close to you experienced a serious illness
____ 5. Suffered the death of someone close
____ 6. Felt grouchy and tense
____ 7. Drank, smoked or ate more than you feel was good for you
____ 8. Experienced financial problems
____ 9. Changed jobs
____ 10. Lost your job
____ 11. Got married
____ 12. Reconciled with your spouse

YOUR PERSONAL STRESSORS

____ 13. Got divorced
____ 14. Separated from your spouse
____ 15. Broke off a seemingly meaningful romantic relationship
____ 16. Experienced an unwanted pregnancy
____ 17. Experienced a desired pregnancy
____ 18. Had an abortion—either spontaneous or induced
____ 19. Experienced dissatisfaction with your physical appearance
____ 20. Experienced dissatisfaction with your professional achievements
____ 21. Were a crime victim
____ 22. Felt overwhelmed by responsibilities
____ 23. Felt you had no time for yourself
____ 24. Were absent minded more often than not
____ 25. Experienced an increase in personal responsibilities
____ 26. Experienced an increase in professional responsibilities
____ 27. Experienced a serious accident
____ 28. Experienced dissatisfaction with your sex life
____ 29. Experienced difficulty concentrating on your work
____ 30. Felt unloved by your family

___ 31. Argued seriously with a family member
___ 32. Felt socially "out of it"
___ 33. Moved from one residence to another
___ 34. Found yourself relying on alcohol, tranquilizers, or other crutches
___ 35. Discovered that your husband or lover was cheating
___ 36. Began an affair
___ 37. Added a member to your household
___ 38. Lost weight without explanation
___ 39. Experienced a business loss, the loss of an investment, or a heavy increase in financial responsibilities
___ 40. Felt that life was meaningless

Count the items that applied to you and write the number on the blank below.

TOTAL: _____

Compare your score with the following ranges.

1-10: This is a LOW score. You appear to have a relatively stress-free environment. What little stress does exist in your life appears to be well-handled.

11-25: This is a MODERATE score. Stress appears to have become a problem in your life and will likely require more attention on your part as to both the particular stressors and your specific stress reactions. Some re-patterning of your life appears requisite. At this level, you may find that several health problems are emerging.

25-40: This is a HIGH score. The large number of stressors that you checked off show you to be susceptible to health and emotional problems. You should make *every* effort to eliminate those sources of stress which are threatening your well-being. In addition, learning to cope with stress is not only desirable at this level *but mandatory*.

How did you do?

If you scored either MODERATE or HIGH on the Compustress form, then you do need help in learning to master your stressors. That's why you are reading this book. Consider where you experience stress, or have experienced stress in the past year. If you checked items one, two, six, nineteen, twenty, twenty-two, twenty-three, twenty-four, twenty-five, twenty-six, twenty-nine, thirty,

thirty-two, or forty, then you have a real need to develop coping skills since these items represent your personal estimate of important stressors. If they are left uncontrolled, they will master you and make your life miserable.

In addition to knowing your stress load, it is also important to know how much you influence and, perhaps, even *invite* stress in your life.

Do you seek out stress? Is a peaceful existence unattractive to you when compared with a life of being constantly "on edge"? Remember the turtle and the race horse personalities. You might be a race horse who strives to live a stress-filled life because a peaceful existence is unthinkable. Such women have been identified as being Type A personalities.

Cardiologists Friedman and Rosenman pointed out in their study of the link between personality and heart disease that the Type A personality is characterized by an intense drive. Aggressiveness, ambition, competitiveness, and pressure for getting work done are her most identifiable features. She has the habit of pitting herself against the clock — or any other competition that is around. Although the Type A may give the impression of being in complete control, she is placing extreme strain on both her mind and her body.

The Type A is always on the move. You have probably recognized quite a few Type A women if you have observed the manner in which different women wait to meet their appointments. The stereotypical Type A is the one who handles take-along business while waiting to see her gynecologist. Her speech is clipped and rushed. Because of the high standards for performance that she sets for herself, Type A drives herself to the extreme and may be hard to get along with. The problem is that she expects similar motivation in others. For the woman who exhibits the Type A, stress-prone personality, every moment of the day is accounted for. There exists no time for play — unless the play is competitive.

Type B, on the other hand, is a more easy-going and relaxing person to spend time with. She glances at her watch infrequently and remains less preoccupied with competitive achievement. This is not to say that she is not interested in success. Rather, the Type B personality is less frantic in her movement toward success. She evidences a more modulated speech pattern than her Type A sister and actually controls her situation more fully.

To be realistic, we must admit that most

women are a mix of the two types. For that reason, most women still need to deal with the stressors of life.

There is one further distinction between the Type A and the Type B personalities which should be made. The behavior pattern of the Type A is closely correlated with the incidence of heart disease. Although we can point to smoking, improper diet, lack of exercise or obesity as underlying causes, the link between a stress-filled life and heart disease is strongly supported and to a greater degree than the relationship with other suspected causes.

What type of personality are you? Are you living a stress-prone life? Is your personality that of a stress-seeker, deliberately creating a climate for stress? Or are you a relaxed and easygoing woman whose life is pretty evenly paced? Are you a turtle or a race horse—or a mixture of both?

Let's take a look at your stress personality patterns and see where your personality falls. To do this, complete the Stress Personality Pattern Evaluation which follows.

STRESS PERSONALITY PATTERN EVALUATION (SPPE)

Instructions: Read each question carefully and fill in the corresponding blank, rating how accurately you feel the question describes you. If you feel that it is *not at all* relevant to your personality, place a 1 in the blank. If it is *somewhat* relevant, than place a 2 in the blank. If the item is *typical* of your personality, than place a 3 in the blank. For instance, if you often rush the last few words of sentences, fill in 3 (typically).

After completing the SPPE, obtain your score by adding all of the numbers that you entered in the blanks. Then look carefully at what those scores mean regarding your personality and life stresses by comparing your score with the scores following the form.

1 — not at all 2 — somewhat 3 — typically

____ 1. Do you move, walk and eat rapidly?
____ 2. Are you impatient with the pace of the world?
____ 3. Do you frequently do two or more things at once?
____ 4. Do you often become involved in several projects at the same time?

_____ 5. Does relaxing and doing absolutely nothing for several hours make you feel guilty?

_____ 6. Do you become irritated out of proportion with others' slowness?

_____ 7. Do you have a habit of looking at your watch or clock often?

_____ 8. Do you emphasize strongly various key words in your speech, even when no real need for this exists?

_____ 9. Do you hurry your sentences along, finishing the last few words as quickly as possible?

_____ 10. Are you preoccupied with your own thoughts?

_____ 11. Are you preoccupied with acquiring material possessions?

_____ 12. Do you feel a chronic sense of having too little time?

_____ 13. Do you have any characteristic gestures or nervous tics?

_____ 14. Do you feel the need to handle every problem alone?

_____ 15. Do you feel that part of your success is due to your ability to do things faster than others?

_____ 16. Are you preoccupied with evaluating your performance and that of others in terms of productivity?

_____ 17. Do you have little time for hobbies or nonproductive (in terms of money) activities?

_____ 18. Are you referred to by others as being "hard-driving"?

_____ 19. When you meet another Type A personality, do you feel little compassion for her affliction?

_____ 20. When you meet another Type A personality, do you feel the need to challenge her?

Let's take a look at your score. Total up the responses and place the number on the line below.

TOTAL: _____

How does it compare with the scores below and the significance which these scores have for both your personality and well-being?

20-25: This is a LOW score. There is definitely no stress problem here. In fact, little stimulation appears to exist in your life which appears to be characterized by nonproductivity. Review the items and make certain that you have responded accurately.

26-40: This is a MODERATE score. From your score, it appears that stress does exist in your life but you also appear to exert some form of control over your stressors. Your life is stimulating, at this point, but care must be taken to *keep* your stressors under control. If you give proper attention to diet and to moderation in your life, the proper balance can be maintained.

41 and above: This is a HIGH score. If your score falls closer to 41, then excessive tenseness is clear and you should begin to take serious measures to control your stressors. If your score appears at the middle to high end of the scale (maximum of 60), then it is time that you acknowledge stress as a significant factor in your life. At this level, your stress personality pattern is endangering both your emotional and physical well-being. As long as you operate in this manner, you remain a serious candidate for the many stress-engendered ills.

Consider the twenty items on the SPPE for a moment. Many of you may have looked at several of the items and said, "That's not unusual. It's just a common aspect of my life." We become so accustomed to functioning at full speed, hurrying along when we could just as effectively walk, that stress becomes a way of life. It is only when we view our lives from a calmer perspective that we see how much of our time is wasted in dangerous preoccupations.

Look at your scores on both the Compustress and the SPPE. Are you in the HIGH category on both? If so, then you are risking your health with each day that you continue your present pattern of behavior. Even if you are in the *moderate,* or acceptable, range, you are bordering on danger unless you begin to take firm control of your life and your stressors. It is too easy for the stressors to become unwieldy and to begin to control you.

In the next few chapters, you will become more aware of your particular stress demons—and of how to exorcise them before seriously embarking on the four-week program. You cannot—and should not—want to *eliminate* stress. Instead, you will learn to harness the energy now stolen from you by stress.

5. Negative Coping Techniques

You have had the opportunity to examine your specific stress load and to assess your unique personality pattern when confronted with stress. Most likely, you were surprised to discover just how high your stress load is and, even more importantly, you were probably astounded by the dangerous patterns you follow in your stress-filled life. The combination of the scores on the Compustress and the Stress Personality Pattern Evaluation should give you an idea of just how important it is for you to start reducing your stress load today!

It is time to explore in greater detail your instinctive physiological and emotional reactions to stress. You will also learn more about the negative coping techniques we sometimes use — frail attempts to deal with our stressors.

A great many women find that stressors stimulate a variety of specific reactions which, in essence, are really our often inadequate attempts to cope with difficult situations. For some of us, the soothing warmth of cup after cup of caffeine-laden coffee creates a temporary euphoria in the midst of a stress-filled day. For others, the temporary "perfect" solution is alcohol. Still others find that chain-smoking cigarettes is the only solution. Certainly, more than one woman has come to believe that she can live through any crisis as long as a plentiful supply of chocolate is near at hand, while another raids her refrigerator with vigor after a particularly stress-filled day. Gulping coffee, drinking, smoking or binging are all attempts to combat the unpleasantries of life. These substances are easily obtained and easily consumed, but the aftereffects are troublesome. Too much of any of these substances creates additional stress in the body, and the results are felt long after the initial stressor has disappeared as we have to cope with our overindulgences. For the drinker or the binger, the morning after can be worse than the original stressor.

NEGATIVE COPING TECHNIQUES

A more serious attempt at coping with stress is the use of prescription drugs which tranquilize, sedate and soothe many women. The relief experienced after taking these medications, however, is only temporary. The original stressors remain. Further, increasing dependence on these substances exacerbates the stressors in a woman's life and creates increasingly difficult stress situations to overcome.

For many of us, the techniques used to cope with stress become habits over the years, much in the same way that stress personality patterns become ingrained as time passes. Associations surround the cup of coffee, the cigarette, the chocolate bar and the valium, giving them an importance all their own in our lives. Instead of seeing their potentially negative effect on our lives, we come to value such substances for their ability to get us through the day.

Do you recognize the way in which you react to stress? Can you identify the crutches upon which you rely when the going gets rough? Do you know whether your attempts at coping have a long-range positive or negative effect on your life?

It's time to know. First, let's take a look at

the variety of stress reactions that exist in your life.

PRESSURE POINTS CHECKLIST

Instructions: Read over each item on this list of characteristic responses of individuals under stress and place an X next to those signs which describe your stress response(s).

____ 1. Pain in the neck or the lower back
____ 2. Frequent need to urinate
____ 3. Excessive perspiring
____ 4. Insomnia
____ 5. Desire to strike out at others
____ 6. Inability to relax
____ 7. Pounding of the heart
____ 8. Feeling of blood rushing to your head
____ 9. Inability to concentrate
____ 10. Headaches which last more than an hour
____ 11. Nervous laughter or giggling
____ 12. Heavy smoking
____ 13. Feeling of disorientation
____ 14. Undefinable fears and anxiety
____ 15. Dryness of the mouth and throat

NEGATIVE COPING TECHNIQUES

_____ 16. Lack of appetite
_____ 17. Compulsive eating
_____ 18. Diarrhea
_____ 19. Indigestion
_____ 20. Queasiness in the stomach
_____ 21. Vomiting
_____ 22. Stuttering
_____ 23. Nervous tics
_____ 24. Uncontrollable urge to cry
_____ 25. Emotional tenseness
_____ 26. Increased smoking
_____ 27. Increased intake of alcohol
_____ 28. Increased use of prescription drugs
_____ 29. Frequent accidents
_____ 30. Nightmares
_____ 31. Grinding of teeth
_____ 32. Pre-menstrual tension
_____ 33. Missed menstrual cycle
_____ 34. Impulsive behavior
_____ 35. Fatigue
_____ 36. Trembling
_____ 37. Frequent loss of temper
_____ 38. Acting edgy and keyed up
_____ 39. Vertigo
_____ 40. Desire to avoid others
_____ 41. Depression
_____ 42. Tendency to be upset by unexpected sounds

____ 43. Anxiety based on no specific cause
____ 44. Skin irritation

Take a close look at the pressure points that you checked. A few are relatively easy to handle. Too many pressure points, however, can be harmful to your mental and physical health. They indicate that your body is not handling stress productively. Because you suspect this already, you are reading this book. If you follow the program, you will become the master of your stress.

Once again, you must know the enemy. Perhaps more importantly, you must become aware of how your body is negatively affected by stressors. Before you can repattern your life, you must know which patterns are harmful and why they are damaging to your body and to your mind.

You have already observed how the body attempts to adapt physiologically to its stressors. As stress continues to build, without relief and without some means of making it work for you, the result is often the gastric ulcer, hypertension, cancer, heart disease and a host of other physical ills.

There are, however, other negative reactions to which we become habituated in our daily response to stress. Some of these reactions, such as subpar performance, depression, anger, anxiety, insomnia, bodily aches and loss or gain of appetite, are clearly detrimental, if involuntary, reactions. Others, such as increased smoking, alcohol intake, drug use (legal and illegal) and caffeine consumption, provide temporary states of euphoria. Thus, they seem beneficial to the individual for the short term, with prolonged use they result in long-term damage.

Voluntary or *involuntary*, these reactions are negative. They are the result of conditioning and may rightly be termed conditioned responses and even habits—bad habits. To improve your response to stress, and to assist you in mastering your stressors, you should understand just what these negative reactions mean to your well being.

At work or at home, when you start to become less efficient it is a clear sign of excessive stress. Stress hampers concentration and your performance suffers. As anxiety over your performance increases, you become even less efficient. These reactions further increase the stress level, trapping you in a vicious cycle. One way to relieve the stress is to lighten the workload, a course which the Type A individual finds especially distasteful. For those who are a combination of Type A and Type B personalities, this is often the only way to alleviate stress and increase performance levels.

There is a variety of involuntary reactions to stress which emerge in our frequently inadequate attempts to deal with the phenomenon. Depression, anxiety, insomnia, physical aches and pains, change of appetite, and anger are some of the most common.

Depression describes a range of moods and a general lack of interest in life. It has been observed to be the most common sign of stress. Simply put, depression is a chronic and low-key feeling of dejection about one's life. Characteristic of depression are sadness, inactivity, lack of energy and an inability to concentrate. Depression is often a generalized response, not linked to a specific calamity or event. Among the most common signs of depression are anxiety, insomnia, the sudden appearance of aches and pains, and a change in appetite. Depressed people are rarely fun to be with — nor do they enjoy their own company.

Anxiety, a symptom of depression, is also a symptom of stress on its own. It is a pervasive, almost physical feeling of apprehension and dread, of being uptight. While fear is the reaction to a specific and often immediate danger, anxiety is concerned with anticipated danger. Anxious people feel unstable. They feel a lack of feedback regarding their performance. They fear the future and believe that they have no effective plans for dealing with what they fear.

Insomnia is a condition too often attributed to everything but the primary cause—stress. Periodic insomnia may be due to excitement regarding the coming day's events (pleasant stress) or anxiety (distress). If insomnia is chronic, then you should realize that this is a danger sign that you are under too much stress. Continuing insomnia signals constant stress, a condition which can be debilitating. To "cure" insomnia, millions of Americans use either alcohol or drugs to relax. What they are saying is that they need something to help them deal with the stress that is making them lose sleep. More will be said later about alcohol and drugs.

Aches and pains of the neck or lower back result from the unconscious tensing of these muscles while we are stressed. Ever feel sore and achy at the end of a day, yet not have engaged in any physical activity on which to blame the pains? Stress is most likely the culprit. When we keep contracting certain muscles as we face stressful situations, they become strained and painful. Thus, one who creates stress in our lives literally becomes for us a "pain in the neck." References to pains of the lower back are also aptly described.

Appetite is a variable among stress responses. Some individuals tend to overeat when under stress while others lose all appetite until calmer times ensue. What is your pattern? Do you lose your appetite when you are under stress? Do you head for the refrigerator, the cupboard, or the ice cream store? Or, do you find that your appetite is unaffected by stress?

For many people, overeating serves as a means of diverting attention from stressors and placing it on food. A great deal of blood is used by a full stomach and intestine. The increased demand for blood in the abdomen produces a slight and temporary tranquilizing effect, caused by less blood circulating in the brain. This reduces mental alertness and attention to stress.

For other women who are feeling stressed, a variety of stress-determined physical disorders, particularly of the stomach, reduces the desire for food. The decline in appetite naturally results in steady weight loss and, if not attended to, can lead to the development of anorexia nervosa. Either way, if you experience an undesired and sudden gain or loss in weight, you should be aware that either of these physical reactions signals excessive stress.

Anger can be both beneficial and detrimental to your physical well-being and to your personal as well as professional relationships. In its most negative sense, anger is exhibited as aggression against anyone and anything. Most often, it is against those we love that we direct anger. Because our families will tolerate our anger, we "dump" on them. Then we feel guilty and uncomfortable because the rational woman inside of us knows that our stress should not be blamed on others. Expressing anger against innocent family members when we are stressed only increases the stress and strains family relationships. Sooner or later, sources of support, affection and love—all badly needed—are cut off or at least lessened. This is especially unfortunate since it is when we appear most angry that we are most in need of love and support.

Anger can also be constructive, however, and aggression should not be feared. Handled properly, aggression can be controlled and channeled to function in a productive manner. We should take a "handle with care" attitude toward reacting with anger to stress. Aggression can be a motivating force which encourages women to overcome obstacles and to eliminate their sources of stress. To be effective, however, aggression and anger must be used in a noncombative manner. It is not the people around us but our stressors which should be attacked and defused. The energies which many women waste in exhibiting anger toward family members and toward themselves could be better used to eliminate their stressors.

In addition to these involuntary reactions to stress which are part of our coping mechanisms, there are several voluntary reactions. These often emerge from conditioning which has built up over years of reacting to stress. Such voluntary reactions are often mistakenly relied upon as quick solutions to the problems of stress. They are, unfortunately, only temporary and they frequently stimulate even greater problems as reliance upon such reactions becomes habitual.

How many times have those of you who smoke told others that you "need" another cigarette because you are nervous, tense or on edge? *Smoking* calms you, or so you claim. Well, aside from its harmful effects on your lungs and other organs of the body, smoking is a good indicator of overstress when the habit shows a steady increase. Although smoking has a temporary calming effect psychologically and physiologically, its long-term effects are just the opposite. The habit further stimulates the body and, thus, increases the severity of the stress response. Nicotine immediately increases the heart rate. In addition, researchers have observed that nicotine also temporarily raises blood pressure and levels of cholesterol and nonadrenaline (closely related to adrenalin). It is logical to conclude, based on these observations, that the more nicotine you take into your body, the greater will be your stress level.

Remember that increased smoking is a sure sign of increased stress and should be viewed as a danger sign. Another stress reaction which is often disguised as a coping mechanism is *drinking*. The consumption of alcohol, particularly an increase in your consumption, is another sign of excessive stress. The tranquilizing effect of liquor is a temporary relief from discomfort which may lead to a severe drinking problem. If you monitor the amount of alcohol you consume, however, your changing intake can be a barometer of excessive stress.

Alcoholism has become a major problem in this nation. As Dr. Aaron T. Beck of the University of Pennsylvania Medical School has observed, once a woman has begun to use a drink as a means of relaxing, the door is opened to increasing numbers of drinks.

Alcohol is involved in a vicious cycle with stress. You have stress, then tension occurs, and then alcohol is consumed to alleviate the stress. Soon alcohol begins to result in further problems which further stress the individual and which lead to greater quantities of alcohol being consumed.

Is alcohol consumption, already a negative means of coping with stress in general, becoming a real problem for you? Why not take a moment to find out. No test or quiz, just respond to the following questions which were formulated by Dr. Harry Johnson of the Medical Board of the Life Extension Institute and which are used to determine the extent of an individual's drinking problem.

1. Do you drink six or more ounces of whiskey a day?

2. Do you always have a couple of cocktails at lunch, even when you are alone?
3. Do you stop for a quick drink at night on the way home from work?
4. Do you habitually order doubles when you drink?
5. Do you sometimes forget to eat after you've had a few drinks?
6. Do you often sneak drinks in the kitchen?
7. Do you start drinking in the morning on weekends?

If you answer yes to more questions than you answer no, it is time to take a long and serious look at what alcohol is doing to you. It is also a serious statement about your life, especially regarding the amount of stress which you are experiencing.

Use of *drugs* to alleviate stress is similarly damaging to your body and mind. As with alcohol, tranquilizers make a woman feel better and may help her to cope temporarily. Feeling better, based on the sense of elation that the pill provides, the individual can get about the business of living. However, drugs teach a woman nothing about dealing with stress — they only mask and further complicate the problem.

You may have been surprised by figures provided in the first chapter regarding the number of anxiety-related drugs prescribed yearly. What follows is even more eye-opening. Focus your attention on the statistics compiled by the New York State Addiction Control Commission in 1970. The Commission interviewed primarily middle-class individuals about their use of drugs, and projected from a sizable sample of the 13.7 million residents of New York State the following use rates. None of the individuals interviewed was a derelict, a flop house resident or a hospital patient.

DRUG USE PREDICTIONS BY THE NEW YORK STATE ADDICTION CONTROL COMMISSION

Barbiturates — 377,000 people in the state dependent on Phenobarbital, Seconal, Tuinal, Amytal, and other depressants of the central nervous system. (Regular use was defined in the survey as six times monthly.)

Sedatives — 173,000 regular users of such medications as Doriden, Noludar, and other non-barbiturates.

Minor tranquilizers—525,000 regular users of Valuium, Librium, Atarax, Miltown, Equanil, Metprotabs and Lobritabel.

Major tranquilizers—Eighty-five thousand regular users of such substances as Stelazine and Mellaril. These drugs are intended for psychotic patients but are given to seemingly normal people to reduce panic, fear and hostility, and to regularize thinking. The eighty-five thousand individuals are defined as "normal."

Antidepressants—Thirty-seven thousand regular users.

Pep pills—110,000 users of amphetamines, dexedrine or benzedrine.

Diet pills—225,000 regular users.

Controlled narcotics—Twenty-one thousand users of opium and methadone.

Methedrine—Thirty-four thousand regular users.

Heroin—Forty-one thousand regular users.

Remember, these figures represent the drug consumption of "average" people. For all of their popularity, pills fail to eliminate stress, and only do further damage by temporarily tranquilizing us. Our senses may be dulled, for a time, but the sources of our stress remain to plague us.

Another negative reaction to stress which is temporarily calming but has long-term bad effects on the body is our intake of *caffeine* through the numerous cups of coffee and soda which we consume. It often appears that the more stress, the greater the caffeine consumption. Many stressed individuals claim that they can't function without their cup of coffee. Their fatigue requires that they have a lift that only coffee can give them. Such dependence is a strain on the body. Increased consumption of caffeine, as with increased consumption of other drugs, including alcohol and nicotine, is a further danger sign of excessive stress.

How does caffeine affect the body physically and psychologically? Coffee drinkers often increase their consumption as their stress loads increase. Each cup of coffee contains an average of from 100 to 150 milligrams of caffeine. As little as only 250 milligrams of caffeine have been linked by researchers to nervousness, insomnia, headaches, sweaty palms, and even ulcers—that is, as few as two cups of coffee a day.

Research has also shown that excessive

amounts of caffeine encourage the same clinical signs in people as those in individuals suffering from anxiety. In short, caffeine encourages stress rather than relieves it.

Negative reactions to stress are often mistaken attempts to cope with the very problem that they aggravate. Unfortunately, they only delay the solutions by tranquilizing the body and lulling us into a false sense of peace. What you must do if you are to effect change in your life should be fairly clear by now. You must understand the nature of your stressors, how they affect you, the manner in which you react to your stressors, and the means which you are currently using to cope with stress. Once you know more about you and stress, then you can begin to deal positively with the problem.

The development of a conditioned stress response and stress personality pattern is not something which occurs overnight. Over years, and after innumerable stress episodes, our minds and bodies develop ways to react to various stressors. This negative patterning becomes gradually ingrained in our behavior and our personalities.

In the same way, learning to deal with stress and to control it also takes time. Conquering stress and making it work for you means re-pat-

NEGATIVE COPING TECHNIQUES

terning your life, changing your habits and developing techniques which will assist you in overcoming the negative effects of stress. The Mastering Stress Program takes these needed changes into account and helps you make stress work for you.

6. So This Is Your Life!

Before getting down to a formal program of learning to master your stressors, let's look at some of the broader aspects of life that inhibit your effective functioning. Remember that your behavior, your habits, and your day-to-day existence are all affected by stress. The stress response, in turn, often has undesirable effects on your health, your personal relationships and your professional performance. It is important to have an overall plan of action which will condition your body and your mind to deal effectively and productively with stress in your total life — not just isolated moments.

You certainly can't avoid stress in life — nor should you attempt to do so. What is necessary is the development of a life style which will condition you to cope effectively when stressed. A few how-to's and dos and don'ts are needed here.

To create a successful life pattern, it is necessary to assess yourself and your life honestly, to slow down and begin easing up in matters which don't really have much significance. Too many of us attempt to be Superwomen whose goals are widespread, whose lives are measured in terms of numbers and of accomplishments rather than in quality, and who are dismayed at anything less than perfection in ourselves. Too much time is spent in the have-to's of life and not enough time is given to the want-to's. To live life as you choose, not life as stress determines its course, you must assert your rights as an individual and avoid wasting time on situations and on individuals who are not deserving of the precious moments allotted to each of us.

Remember, stressors which plague us and which render our lives miserable are not created solely by external forces. Many times, we are our own worst enemies. Self-stress, caused by personal perceptions and responses to changes in our lives, situations and circumstances, is a critical factor in our well-being.

Such self-induced stress is a vital element in determining our personal stress threshold.

There are at least three ways in which we needlessly and endlessly increase anxiety in our lives. Most of us fall into at least one of these three roles if we are having a difficult time with stress:

1. *The "Awfulizer"* — This woman views events, situations or circumstances as being catastrophic and unbearable. The complete pessimist, the awfulizer refuses to see any good in any stress situation and is usually prepared for the worst. As a result of her expectations, the awfulizer often finds that she is subject to the worst fate possible.

2. *The "Should – er"* — This woman spends her time demanding that others should be different than the way they are, or that the world should be different. Her communication, however, is often silent and takes place in her thoughts. The should-er rarely makes any move to right the wrongs in her world and, instead, just complains that things should be more fair, more just, more easy, etc.

3. *The "Generalizer"* — The generalizer condemns herself or others solely on a single performance or on one set of behaviors or traits. You will often hear the generalizer wailing, "I'm a failure" or "I'm worthless because I was fired" or "I let my family down." The condemnation is strong but no meaningful action is taken to correct the perceived deficiency.

Do these roles sound familiar? If they do, then your stress may be self-induced. On the other hand, you may perceive the stress situations in your life as being primarily external.

Whether your stressors are internal or external, you will benefit from developing and practicing good mental and physical health as a means of conquering stress. Most of us try too hard to excel, even to the point of establishing unrealistic goals, then we suffer in the stress situations which result.

There are a number of ways in which we can successfully reorder our lives. Examine the Guides for Repatterning which follow. Note how strongly the emphasis is placed on your goals, on you controlling events in your life so as to gain the maximum mastery over stress.

Guides for Repatterning

1. Set realistic goals.
2. Establish personal targets, adapted to your particular pace.
3. Avoid conflicting goals.
4. Don't try so hard that your performance begins to deteriorate under the pressure of excessive strain.
5. Avoid rigidity, in both your professional and personal life.
6. Don't be deterred by failure. Accept setbacks as being a part of life.
7. Learn to say no, tactfully but forcefully.
8. Don't overload your day with work (once again, be realistic in goal-setting).
9. Live one day at a time and learn to cope with your allotted tasks for one twenty-four hour period at a time.
10. Establish a system of priorities.
11. Set aside time for reflection.
12. Tackle decision-making in an orderly manner.
13. Don't procrastinate.
14. Skip the post-mortems and self-recrimination.
15. Learn to assert yourself firmly.
16. Live in the present.

For too many women, the many remonstrations to be more assertive in our lives amount to a major reorganization of thinking. We, too often, find ourselves saying yes when we really mean no. Goals are permitted to become burdens rather than desired outcomes, and priorities develop based on the whims of others rather than on our own choices.

To follow a life style which reflects the Guides for Repatterning may seem difficult. And it is difficult — at first. It is difficult because most of us are used to living our lives as subjects of stressors, both internal and external. Breaking free of that tyranny requires substantial effort — but it is certainly worth it.

There are two parts to any approach to stress management: the long-term consideration and the short-term technique. To truly master stress, you must re-pattern your life to encourage the development of strong defenses and to lessen needless stress in your life.

Among the long-term changes that are needed are the following: (1) clarification of your values and goals; (2) development of a secure self-image; (3) development of good mental and physical health habits; (4) adherence to a policy of time management. A life guided by these principles will be more evenly paced, healthier, and less subject to unproductive stress.

Short-term techniques for dealing with isolated and powerful stress incidents are also vital as they teach us to cope with the inevitable stressors which invade our daily lives. These techniques make up the Mastering Stress Program which appears later. For now, let us examine the variety of ways to prevent the stressors of life from conquering us. Let us engineer a life for ourselves which is less stress-filled and more tranquil.

CLARIFYING YOUR VALUES

Clarifying your values is not merely an exercise in sorting out random thoughts but a way of providing stability and security in this world, which holds too many surprises and shocks for women. Making certain that your life is in harmony with your values *does* help to reduce stress. If you live at cross-purposes with your values or ideals, your stress level increases as conflicting values inevitably emerge. Ask yourself the following questions, and write in the answers in the space provided.

SO THIS IS YOUR LIFE!

1. What is truly important to me?

   _____
   _____
   _____
   _____

2. What is the value of my life?

   _____
   _____
   _____
   _____

3. What in my life is worth dying for?

   _____
   _____
   _____
   _____

4. What would an outsider see as being my life values, if she were only to observe my activities?

   _____
   _____

SO THIS IS YOUR LIFE!

_____

_____

5. What does my checkbook indicate as being important to me?

_____

_____

_____

_____

6. Is my daily way of life consistent with my perceived goals?

_____

_____

_____

_____

7. Do I have important goals? What are they?

_____

_____

_____

_____

If you give serious thought to your specific values and goals, and if you attempt to make your life activities reflect these goals, then harmony will emerge in your life. In establishing a stable base, you will develop a better foundation from which to manage your stressors.

DEVELOPMENT OF A SECURE SELF-IMAGE

You develop a secure self-image when you know where you are going and what you want to do when you get there. Every woman has a specific stress threshold which she cannot exceed without suffering great physical and psychological pain. But the better your self-image, the better you will be able to stand up to stress.

Improving your self-image takes a concentrated effort. Two basic psychological needs determine how we feel about ourselves: the need to love and be loved; and the need to feel worthwhile to ourselves and to others. If these two needs are met, then we are better able to develop a healthy self-image. Everyone needs to be wanted and wants to be needed.

Primarily, you have to assess just what you are doing in life. Is your life meaningful to you? How does it connect with your goals and values? In essence, self-image is not only a product of how others view you but, more importantly, of how you view yourself. If you are living a life which contradicts the values and goals in which you believe, then stress is a natural outcome. If you are experiencing stress in regard to self-image, it may be time to alter your life, to assess what it is you want and to go out and accomplish your goals. You may have to lose a little to gain a lot. The gain, however, is substantial since it consists of control over your own life.

GOOD MENTAL HEALTH HABITS

Good mental health habits are important long-term aids in helping us manage stress and keep strong when sudden stressors appear. The well-adjusted person is better able to deal with stress. Following are seven rules which have been recognized for many years as important to healthy psychological adjustment. They are an excellent guide to arming ourselves psychologically.

1. *Learn to accept yourself*—Realize that you are not perfect and never will be. That doesn't mean you can't improve. But you have to accept all of your strengths and weaknesses, your failures and successes.

You are the only "you" that you have. Perfect or otherwise, there is no other raw material for the person you would like to be. But, never denigrate the individual who exists at present. Just decide to improve.

2. *Have someone to trust and to talk with* — A confidante is an invaluable means of reducing stress. All of us need a sounding board and sympathetic listeners. Unfortunately, some of us view confiding in others as a sign of weakness. It isn't. It is a valuable stress reducer.

3. *Act constructively to eliminate your sources of stress* — Do something about what continues to generate tension in your life. If the source of stress is personal, talk with the individual who is initiating your stress. If the problem is professional, find a new job or even a new career.

4. *Vary your acquaintances* — Don't socialize only with the people with whom you work or only with other Type A personalities. Try to cultivate friendships with women in other professional fields, and those

whose life styles are more relaxed than yours.

5. *Vary your activities* — All work and no play not only makes a woman dull but it can give her ulcers, hypertension or heart disease. Hobbies, vacations, short respites from your daily schedule and other changes are necessities in everyone's life. Such variations help to offset stress and add interest to life.

6. *Use the scientific management method of problem-solving to regulate your life* — Learn to view problems, both personal and professional, from a rational, problem-solving standpoint. The scientific management method has four steps. Identify the problem, come up with several possible solutions, analyze the alternatives, and make a decision based on the analysis.

7. *Maintain good physical health* — This final point will be discussed in greater detail because it drastically affects our ability to cope effectively with stress. Maintaining good physical health means giving attention to both nutrition and to the physical condition of our bodies. Being in good

physical condition increases our resistance to physical and psychological stressors and gives us resilience when faced with stress.

NUTRITION AND EXERCISE

Poor nutrition is responsible for a wide number of diseases, including hardening of the arteries, diabetes, hypertension and heart disease. The excessive intake of fat, sugar, salt, cholesterol and caffeine which characterizes our national diet has been cited by the medical profession as being largely responsible for many of our physical ills.

High levels of cholesterol in our diet join with serum cholesterol which is activated by stress to make many of us walking time bombs.

Sugar, consumed by Americans at an average of 126 pounds per year, leads to a number of health problems: obesity, tooth decay, diabetes, high levels of blood fat, and arteriosclerosis. Simple sugars such as honey increase a blood fat called triglycerides. Blood triglycerides, like blood cholesterol, are associated with heart disease, since they trigger adrenalin flow. Thus, they sabotage the already stressed body's defense mechanism.

Salt leads to the development of hypertension, and to its aggravation. Yet, many of us consume great amounts of junk foods laden with salt.

Another damaging food substance is caffeine, already discussed. In addition to its ability to make us tense and edgy, caffeine has another damaging effect: It increases the amount of free fatty acids in the blood. This is extremely dangerous to the stressed individual who may already be on the way to a heart attack.

Eating well is by itself not enough to succeed in coping with stress. Exercise is equally important. Although specific exercises may alleviate stress-related tension in particular parts of the body, exercise as part of a regular regimen is extremely valuable. Not only does exercise firm up the body but it performs the following functions in helping us to deal more effectively with stress:

1. It reduces our level of anxiety.
2. It provides an acceptable form of letting off steam.
3. It builds up stamina.

4. It counteracts the biochemical effects of stress.
5. It reduces the risk of psychological illness.

Most of the above are self-explanatory, but the fourth statement bears further examination. When we are placed in a stress-filled situation, our pulse races, blood pressure soars, and the stress hormones adrenalin and nonadrenaline pour into our bodies. In the process, these stress hormones release sugar and fatty acids — the fuels of muscular activity — into our blood streams. Since these are not burned up by a violent physical reaction in our civilized society, they tend to be deposited in the blood vessel walls. There, they form the basis for arteriosclerosis and coronary disease. Exercise functions to eliminate this buildup. Therefore, not only can exercise help to alleviate tension, but it can also reverse the harmful effects of stress.

A note of warning: If you are not in good overall physical condition, then exercise can do more harm than good to your body. The best way to start any exercise program is to see a doctor first for a thorough physical checkup. Tell her what you plan to do and let her know the extent of the exercise program. Not only is the physical checkup vital, but you should also be certain to have an electrocardiogram stress test. Even after all of this, you should take it easy at first. Don't overexert yourself.

One quick way to tell if you are in good condition is to take the following test. Sit quietly for about five minutes. Now, take your pulse. The wrist is most frequently used, but a more effective method is pressing your thumb against the carotid artery in the side of the neck. Check the beat against the sweep of the second hand of your clock or watch for a full sixty seconds. If the heart at rest beats at eighty times a minute or more, then you *are not* in good condition. If your heart at rest beats at sixty beats a minute or fewer, then your condition is good. A little above seventy beats a minute is average.

To be certain, take your pulse four or five times in different resting situations, and then take the average.

Once again, while nutrition and exercise are important in relieving stress, both must be approached with care. Good nutrition should consist, simply enough, of a well-balanced diet which includes the four food groups: fruits and vegetables, meat, dairy products, and grains and cereals. Two servings daily of meat and dairy products are sufficient, and four or more servings of the other two categories round out your diet. For women, the loss of iron during menstruation often means that an iron supplement is required, even if you eat iron-rich foods. If your diet is well-balanced, and draws upon all four food groups in appropriate measure, you don't need megadoses of vitamins.

An exercise regimen should be well-planned to deal not only with stressors in general but to give attention to specific parts of the body. Tense neck, shoulder, back and leg muscles are painful manifestations of stress. Exercise in these areas not only unties the knots but helps drive stress away. It is also a good idea to exercise those parts of your body which you feel need work because dissatisfaction with physical appearance is an important source of stress to most women.

LEARN TO RELAX

Even if we give attention to all of the active means of combatting stress, such as clarifying our values, setting goals, eating correctly, and exercising adequately, there remains the need to allow our bodies to relax in order to relax our minds. In managing stress, learning to relax is extremely important.

Popular magazines are full of quick tips for relaxing. They advocate taking a hot bath, playing soft music, and other, less convenient and temporary routes toward relaxation. The fads of yoga, hypnosis, transcendental meditation, autogenics, and biofeedback have come and gone. In essence, the intention of all of these techniques is relaxation. Even self-hypnosis, with its emphasis on auto-suggestion as a means of changing behavior, strives to bring the body to a point of relaxation and to calm the mind.

A technique advanced by Dr. Herbert Benson of the Harvard Medical School contains the essence of all forms of meditation in eliciting the relaxation response. It is made up of four basic components: (1) a quiet place; (2) selection of a word; (3) a passive attitude; and (4) placing oneself in a comfortable seated position with eyes closed.

The process of relaxation is not merely a passive act. It is an exercise in which you gain mastery over the process of attention and, thus, mastery over stimuli. When you relax successfully, there is a temporary shutdown of the information-processing mechanisms of the brain which often stimulate stress.

The drawing out of the relaxation response from the body helps to counteract the fight-or-flight response by bringing about a series of biochemical changes. Although regular and scheduled relaxation, whether or not you are stressed, can be beneficial if practiced two or three times daily, the relaxation response is especially valuable when you are confronted with a particularly stressful situation.

Numerous research studies have shown that a variety of physiological changes occur due to consistent practice of the relaxation response:

1. Oxygen consumption decreases.
2. Respiratory rate decreases.
3. Heart rate decreases.
4. Alpha brain waves (signifying a more relaxed state) increase.
5. Blood pressure decreases.
6. Muscle tension decreases.

In short, the relaxation response de-stresses or unstresses the body. Remember that meditation, yoga, biofeedback, or any other relaxation technique remains *only a part* of learning to cope with stress. Mastering stress requires a total program of learning.

Now, practice the relaxation response. Sit quietly and make yourself as comfortable as possible. Close your eyes. Select a word or phrase to repeat over and over again in your mind. You can use the word "one" as Benson suggests, or any other one-syllable word — any word or sound will do. It is the total concentration on the word that is important. Keep your eyes closed and concentrate on your sound.

Begin to breathe slowly through your nose. Become aware of the rhythm of your breathing as you silently repeat your word. Continue this for about ten minutes.

After the ten minutes have passed, open your eyes slowly and feel how relaxed your body has become. If you feel little change the first time that you try the relaxation response, don't become discouraged. You are probably unfamiliar with such attempts at relaxing and your body will have to become accustomed to the activity. After a few tries, you will begin to notice several physical changes.

Think about the experience for a moment after each relaxation session. Try to answer the following questions for yourself. Did you relax at all? Can you describe what you felt? Did your heart speed up in the first few moments? Any other changes? Record your responses on the lines below so that you can compare your early experiences with the relaxation response to later attempts, once your body has become accustomed to the feeling.

_____
_____
_____
_____
_____ .

Incorporate the relaxation exercise into your daily routines. You can practice the relaxation exercise on a plane, the train, the bus, at home or in the library. Practice two to three times daily, allowing approximately twenty minutes for each relaxation session. Postpone the exercise to at least two hours after eating because the digestion process inhibits total relaxation.

Managing stress requires that you also learn to manage your life more effectively. We have reviewed a variety of ways in which change or modification of your life style may be necessary. Being in good physical condition is important in dealing successfully with stress.

Understanding how the way you *do* live conflicts with the way you *want* to live affects your ability to handle stress. Learning to manage your life is a way of telling the world and yourself that you are taking control. It is in this last area that many of us are the weakest. In addition to improving your self-image and clarifying your values, you must also learn to effectively manage time.

TIME MANAGEMENT

How you use your time is very important in your defense against stress. Have you ever stopped to think about how you spend your days? Take a moment and, in the blank preceding each activity in the following list, indicate the amount of time (expressed in hours and parts of an hour) spent in each activity during a normal day. Note that some categories overlap (for instance, eating and business lunches). When you get to the last two items "Total hours spent under stress" and "total stress-free hours," remember that which activities are stressful or stress-free is an entirely individual matter. Perhaps part of the time you spent with your husband/boyfriend is stressful and part is stress-free. Sleeping sounds like a stress-free category, but those of you suffering from insomnia or nightmares may decide that three of your eight sleeping hours were stressful. Don't take any of your activities for granted.

TIME MANAGEMENT CHART

Time Spent

_____ 1. Sleeping
_____ 2. Eating
_____ 3. Working at your job (include work taken home and business lunches)
_____ 4. Relaxing and doing *nothing* else
_____ 5. Taking care of yourself (include dressing, putting on makeup, showering and exercising)
_____ 6. Housekeeping (include meal preparation)
_____ 7. Taking care of children
_____ 8. Spending time with your husband/boyfriend
_____ 9. Entertaining yourself (include reading, watching television, listening to music, and any hobbies)
_____ 10. Shopping

SO THIS IS YOUR LIFE!

____ 11. Traveling (include commuting time)
____ 12. Socializing with friends
____ 13. Other (specify)_____
____ TOTAL STRESSFUL HOURS*
____ TOTAL STRESS-FREE HOURS*

*The two need *not* add up to 24 hours.

Review your breakdown for the day. Are you surprised at the variety of divisions in your day? Are you at the job more than you sleep? Do you spend less time relaxing than you do housekeeping? What about the number of hours spent under stress in a day? Is all of that bad stress or do you consider a portion of that stress to be benficial?

When you examine how fast, productive, stressful and satisfying your life is, you develop a useful means of reducing the damage of stress. Every woman should sit down periodically to examine her pace of life.

Look at how you manage time. Consider your life style as you answer the following questions:

1. Is your present pace of life comfortable for you? Why or why not?

_____

_____

_____

_____

2. Are you trying to do too much? If the answer is yes, list the areas in which you consider yourself overburdened.

_____

_____

_____

_____

3. Are you constantly pressing beyond your stress threshold? How? Why?

_____

_____

_____

_____

4. Are you doing the things you want to do, or are you always attempting to please others and not yourself? In what ways are you pleasing others?

SO THIS IS YOUR LIFE!

_____

_____

_____

_____

5. Are you attending social functions out of obligation rather than with an eye toward having fun? If so, list several social functions in the past year which fit into this category.

_____

_____

_____

6. Are you accepting invitations which you would rather decline? If so, why?

_____

_____

_____

_____

7. Where could you save time, and thus reduce stress, in your schedule by eliminating specific activities?

_____

_____

_____

_____

The preoccupation with time, characteristic of many women who are under stress, amounts to a "hurry sickness." Such women rush around, taking on far more than their fair share of responsibility and attempting to do everything themselves. In many instances, this obsession to hurry results in a far more serious physical sickness, that of heart disease. Of course, other stress-related diseases, such as cancer, hypertension, diabetes and so on, are also undesirable possibilities. When the body finally succumbs to one of the stress-related diseases, the need to keep moving becomes frustrated as the downed woman finds herself directing her life from a hospital bed — not a desirable alternative.

Before that threat becomes a reality, why not attempt to minimize stress by adopting specific strategies for living? The following general guidelines can effectively reduce your "hurry sickness" and aid you in cutting down stress.

RULES FOR RECLAIMING YOUR TIME

1. *Don't permit time to rule you* — Watching the clock constantly increases your tension and is of little worth in any practical sense. Traffic moves no faster and neither do store clerks when you glare at your watch. Fretting about lost time does nothing to change the situation. The constant race with time leads to increased tension, fatigue and accidents, but no real improvement in performance. We suffer needless frustration as we try to force change in the natural course of events. Certainly, not all of us can be as offhanded as former mayor of New York, Jimmy Walker, who, when criticized for arriving late for a public dinner, remarked: "If you're there before it's over, you're there on time." Only a public dinner, perhaps, but this comment is enlightening.

   Does a minute more or less, or an hour more or less, make a difference in a particular situation? In some cases it may. But if your entire day is lived striving to keep to a schedule, you are in need of a reassessment. Some appointments must be kept to the moment. Some may be broken, delayed or changed. You must look long and hard at your schedule, and determine into which of these categories your appointments fall. In some cases, you may find that there is extreme wisdom in letting life develop at its own pace. Regard the following Taoist maxim: "Don't push the river, let it flow."

2. *Work according to your own rhythm* — An aid in doing this is to pace yourself to spread your work over more time, rather to compress it into a short period with no break along the way. Categorize, if you have to, and make your workload *comfortable* rather than burdensome.

3. *Learn to control the way in which your time is spent* — Look at your time-management list and consider the activities which were omitted. How can you reapportion your time? You have to set realistic goals for yourself, ones which can be met without creating stress. Once these goals have been set, you must work steadily toward achieving them. Establish definite time blocks, then adjust them as you find ac-

tivities that are more or less worthy of allotted time.

4. *Allow some free time in the day's schedule* — A filled appointment book allows for all sorts of foul-ups which can lead to stress. Plan on doing a reasonable amount of work, or anything else. However, leave room in the schedule for overrun of activities. Allow yourself time to breathe. You have to start thinking of your health as important, and relaxation is critical to maintaining your health. Where might you schedule one or two relaxation periods each day?

5. *Live in the present* — This is more important than you might believe at this point. Worrying about the present is work enough for most of us without the attendant worries about past failures and the future.

6. *Concentrate your efforts* — Time-wasting, stress-producing interruptions must be eliminated if you are to make maximum use of scheduled time. Tell others that you will call them back. Take the phone off the hook. Tell your secretary to hold all calls until a specific time.

7. *Learn to say no whenever possible* — You don't have to be cruel or harsh in your refusal. Instead, you must be honest in refusing to participate in activities or to take on responsibilities which will burden you unnecessarily. Your time is important to you and to those you love. You have to save time to take part in desired activities. Saying no, kindly but firmly, reclaims such time for you.

The point is that you have to take control of your life and of your schedule as much as possible to defeat the stressors which missed appointments, crowded days and encroaching deadlines stimulate.

But as valuable as it is in coping with stress, time management alone is not the key. Nor is clarification of values and goals or developing a secure self-image. And while good mental health and nutrition and a conditioned body are all important, none of these in themselves can make you master of your stressors.

Following these principles will provide you with a life which is more evenly paced, healthier and, thus, less subject to unproductive stress. However, stress will never be totally eliminated, nor should we want it to be. Remember that stress results from both good (happy marriage, desired birth, promotions, raises, awards) and bad stressors (unhappy marriage, undesired birth, demotions, firings, criticism). Stress is the result of change, and change is essential to human existence. A life without change is not life.

7. Dealing with the Inevitables

Expect stress. As you follow the principles discussed thus far, and the four-week program to come, you will notice that it is your reaction or response to stress that will change. Events won't get to you as they did before. A change in priorities, a firm belief in your goals and a new awareness of your values will make you more confident. When you know where you're going, less is likely to throw you off course.

Still, a certain amount of stress (and no one knows just how much!) will continue to infest your life. To deal with these inevitable incidents, here is a program that will provide you with a variety of short-term techniques (as opposed to the long-term techniques detailed earlier in this book).

Family tensions, jobs, financial strains and the like can't be willed away. Even a life lived according to the preventive techniques can be thrown off course by stress in these areas. Daily threats to our person (drunks in the park, crossing a crowded street, just entering the subway) elevate our susceptibility to stressors and often result in a stressful situation.

What are your options in dealing with these inevitable stressors? Because you have been reading this book, you know that you shouldn't just fall back into bad stress habits to cope with stressors. You don't begin grinding your teeth, or tensing your muscles (unless it is for the purpose of relaxing them). You don't take a drink, pills or other escape potion. You don't begin gnawing at your fingernails, your pencil or your desk. *None of these is the right response.* Instead, you look for a means of managing your stress.

Remember, once again, that it is how you perceive your stressor that determines how intense your reaction will be. Certainly, stress is not just all in the mind, but thinking about the situation clearly will help minimize your bad response — and the damage to your physical and emotional being.

Following are three rules to memorize for use when faced by stressors that are unavoidable:

1. *Don't merely say, "I can't handle it" then bury your head in the sand* — Instead, keep mentally alert and think in detail about the stress-causing situation. Clear analysis will result in a better understanding of just what is plaguing you — and how to deal with the stress situation.

2. *Don't lose your head* — However unsettling the stressor, convoluted thinking only makes it worse. Allowing your thinking to become confused will only make you act irrationally. Your stress increases as irrational thinking decreases your ability to deal effectively with stress.

3. *Remember that the situation will not last forever* — Your in-laws will eventually leave. The boss will relent. You will get another job. This may sound like a variation on thinking positively, and it may well be. But, more importantly, it is a reminder

that stress is finite. That alone makes it potentially manageable.

If you keep a cool head and examine the stress situation calmly, you will find that you always have options in dealing with stress. Depending on your perception of the situation, you can choose to *tolerate the stress*, knowing that it will eventually go away and leave you none the worse for wear. You can arm yourself mentally and choose to *fight* the stressor. Or you can *retreat* from the stress-causing situation.

A careful, clear-headed look at your stressors will tell you which choice is best.

Let's look at an example. Assume that you are working for a company where layoffs are rumored. The grapevine says that your department, along with five others, will be severely cut back. Certainly, among all but the independently wealthy, this is enough to throw anyone into a tailspin. How might you deal with it?

You can choose to tolerate your stressors and wait for the rumors to become reality. You'll probably receive adequate warning to go job-hunting. No use getting ulcers over it.

Or you can take the offensive and approach the brass directly with inquiries. You could sniff around for indications, pump others for information, and spend much of your work time looking out for your future.

Your third choice is to avoid the pain entirely and to begin job-hunting immediately. You can retreat. Even if you are happy at the company, instead of waiting and worrying, you could find another job and resign from the present one. Therefore, you will be secure and sure.

Three choices and each appears viable. However, depending upon the given situation, any of the three could be right — or wrong.

In taking a wait-and-see approach, you may wait too long. As time rolls on, you will become more anxious if the rumors continue. Thus, unless you can wait and take the consequences of not knowing for sure, this approach wouldn't work for you.

In taking the offensive, there exist other pitfalls. The rumors may be just rumors. But by sniffing around and worrying, you will increase your stress. You will also weaken your own position in the company, thus causing the stress to increase further and with good reason. If the rumors are true, then a fight approach might be appropriate. But, if they

DEALING WITH THE INEVITABLES

aren't, just how much will your aggressiveness help?

Sounding the retreat may seem to be a good idea at the time. Why wait until the ax falls? Better to get yourself a new job, even if it is one which you like less, which pays less and which has less convenient hours. Make sense? Not really — unless the rumor is true and no equivalent employment is in sight. Such a retreat guarantees not only a continuation of stress but the possibility of increased and intensified stress in a new job which has little going for it.

Is this to say that no solution is correct? Somewhat. The only correct solution is the one which follows a careful look at your stressors and some clear thinking about your options — and the repercussions of these options. Each stress situation must be viewed individually before a decision can be made. The point is that once the mysterious nature of the stressor is revealed, eliminating stress becomes a problem to be solved logically and rationally.

But how do you eliminate the effects of stressors upon your body and mind? A number of physical and cognitive strategies are useful in coping with stress situations.

1. *Take a walk* — Walking, often looked at as a way of avoiding stress, is also a way of getting rid of built-up tension and releasing our bodies and minds from the grip of stress.

2. *Exercise* — Do jumping jacks. Jump rope. Do push-ups, chin-ups or whatever movement drains your body of the stress-induced tenseness and stiffness. Let the flow of adrenalin be used to push your body in exercise rather than to create stomach acid that gives you ulcers, or to encourage the creation of serum cholesterol, which can damage your heart.

3. *Massage those tightened muscles* — Is your neck often tense? An effective way to eliminate such tension is to reach behind your neck and to grasp it with your hand. Knead slowly and gently at first. As you become more accustomed to the kneading, work the knots out more vigorously.

   Lower back a problem? Place both hands on your lower back, thumbs at waist and fingers outstretched against the back. Using your thumbs to grip, begin manipulating your back with the outstretched fingers and press hard.

What about shoulders? Massage those muscles.

Naturally, a thorough, all-over massage is best. For this, you need a licensed masseuse or a willing-to-learn partner. Most health clubs or spas have licensed personnel as part of their services. Some reputable hotels also offer massage therapists as part of their pool-and-sauna packages.

4. *Stretch*—Stretching doesn't just mean the little movement of the body when we yawn. Stretch deliberately. Reach for the ceiling. Raise your hands straight toward the ceiling. Reach with one upstretched hand as if you were grasping air. Then the other hand. Alternate grasping for air.

Now move to the count of 1-2-3-4. (Do this set of four for a few times.) Can you feel the muscles of your lower back stretching? Feel the tension leaving your sides? Feel the pull in your rib cage? It's good for you.

For tension in the shoulders, do a classic warm-up exercise. Sit up straight with your hands resting in your lap. Lift your shoulders toward your ears. Now roll your shoulders forward. Roll them to the original raised position. Let your shoulders drop. Lift your shoulders again. Now, roll them backward. Back again to the original raised position. Drop your shoulders. Feel the stretch? Try this the next time that your shoulders feel tense.

What about your neck? Another good warm-up exercise (used in dancing, exercise spas and yoga) is the neck roll. Sit up straight, with your hands in your lap. (1) Drop your head forward and let your chin rest on your chest. (2) Lift your head and drop it on your right shoulder. (3) Lift your head and drop it back. (4) Lift your head and drop it on your left shoulder. Bring your head back to position one. Now, go through the four positions without lifting your head each time. Roll your head from your chest, to your shoulder, to the back, to the shoulder, to the chest again, while you count mentally or out loud.

You will probably have difficulty at first, unless your body is accustomed to exercise. Do you feel a pull back down your shoulder blades? Those are stiff muscles which should be limber. If you practice the neck roll for a week or two, you'll soon find your neck muscles will be flexible. After this, doing a neck roll when your tenseness centers in the neck during stress will be highly effective.

All of these stretches can be done at your desk or anywhere else you might be seated. If you are alone, or don't feel inhibited, you can stand and stretch upward as you did while seated. You can also touch your toes and stretch in that way. Swing your arm, from an outstretched position, back and forth. Put your hands on your hips and twist your upper torso to the right and to the left. Do this several times.

All of these stretches, and others which you might think of, help you to cope with stress by alleviating some of the accumulated tension.

5. *Do the Muscle Relaxation Exercise* — Lie down on a carpeted surface or your bed. You will be tensing every part of your body, so make certain that the surface beneath you is comfortable and not too hard. Play soothing music to further relax your mind as you do the exercise.

Now, begin to tense every part of your

body, one portion at a time, following instructions.

Tighten up the muscles of your toes, curling them up with all of your strength. Next, tense your ankle muscles. Keep these muscles tense while you slowly tighten the calf muscles, feeling the strain as you proceed. Feel the effort in maintaining the tenseness of your muscles. Now, tighten the muscles of your knees, then your thighs. Slowly tighten the muscles of your buttocks, feeling the tension which arises as you strain to tighten all of your lower body.

Moving slowly upward, concentrate on your stomach muscles. Feel them pull in toward your spine as you tighten the stomach. Now the rib cage. Tense your shoulders. Tighten the muscles in your fingers. Concentrate on your arms. Tense your arm muscles and feel the muscles pull at your flesh. Move upward to the muscles in your neck, and tighten them as you also begin to squint and tighten your facial muscles.

Most of the muscles in your body are now tightened and they should feel as if they are straining to be allowed to relax.

Don't let them. Hold your muscles tensed for one full minute.

After a minute, you will slowly relax each muscle individually, in a direction opposite to the one used in tensing the muscles.

Relax the muscles of the forehead first, then allow the muscles in your cheeks to go slack. Stop squinting. Now relax your neck. Feel the relief as your shoulders are permitted to fall slowly downward. Let the muscles of your arms and fingers untense.

Turn your attention to the middle portion of your body. Loosen your stomach muscles, then relax the muscles in your rib cage. At this point, your buttocks muscles must be straining mightily. Let them relax. Now, concentrate your attention on your legs which are the only parts of your body that should now be tight. Relax your thighs. Feel the tightness leave the muscles, now loosen the muscles in the knees. Slowly free the muscles in the calves, and experience the relief as the tenseness leaves. Finally, untense the muscles in your ankles and in your toes.

All of the muscles in your body should

now be relaxed. There should be no tightness in your neck and no stiffness in your shoulders. Keep your eyes closed for a few moments while you inhale deeply through your nose (mouth closed), then exhale deeply through your mouth, emptying your lungs totally. Do this four times.

Remember to tense each muscle as hard as you can. You should imagine that you are trying to squeeze the stress out of your muscles and out of your body.

6. *Do Deep Breathing* — For a moment, sit up in your seat and do this exercise. Breathe in deeply through your nose and exhale thoroughly through your mouth. Ready? All right. Breathe in. Hold the breath as you count silently to five. Exhale slowly. Breathe in. Hold. Exhale. Do this five times or more.

7. *Do the Relaxation Response Exercise* — Sit quietly and make yourself as comfortable as possible. Close your eyes. Select a word or phrase to repeat over and over again in your mind. Use any one-syllable word or sound. It is the total concentration on the sound that is important. Keep your eyes closed and concentrate on your sound.

Begin to breathe slowly in through your nose. Pay attention to the rhythm of your breathing as you silently repeat your sound. Continue this for ten minutes.

After ten minutes have passed, slowly open your eyes and feel how relaxed your body has become. Think about the experience after each session and note as you achieve deeper states of relaxation.

Use this procedure to relieve stress, and as an insurance against stressors.

All of these physical approaches are valuable in coping with stress situations. They alleviate the tension caused by stressors and clear the mind to allow us to think of alternatives.

In addition, there are several strategies which may be used in *managing* the stress situation. In the case of known stressors, the best way to learn to manage them is to practice in advance. If you know that certain stressors always get you — be they your boss, social functions or relatives — then you can learn to master them. All it takes is a little imagining. Remember earlier in this book where you were asked to identify a stress situation, the stressors, your reactions and your attempts at coping?

Pick out a familiar stress situation, one which occurred recently. Analyze it. Was it avoidable? What was the specific stressor in the situation? How might your reaction differ in the future, once you see the stressor beginning to act? Can you use a better coping technique than in the past now that you know more about stress? Is it possible that you can eliminate the stressor — or stress reaction — altogether through use of your new knowledge? If not, don't be concerned.

What of the unknown, unrecognized or unexpected stressors which bombard our lives every day? Approach them rationally. First, try to identify your stressor in a particular situation. If an impending job interview, confrontation, meeting or other activity is making you fearful, rehearse the scene. Run through the job interview in advance. Practice potential questions, gestures, comments. Mentally familiarize yourself with what is to come.

In a particularly stressful situation, you might also try mentally talking to yourself. Create coping statements and repeat them silently to yourself. These are useful not only in preparing for a stressful situation, but in dealing with feeling overwhelmed in the middle of a stressful experience. For example, as you face an irate customer, boss, co-worker, child, parent or other relative, you might keep in mind the following: "I know it will soon be over. She (he) is angry about _____ and needs to get it all out. Things have been worse."

When you face a critical interview, keep in mind that this is not the first interview you've had. You've made it through others and you will make it through this interview, too.

The same silent talk with yourself works in personal situations. All it is, basically, is a means of feeding yourself positive reinforcement.

Self-statement works as a guide, a means of keeping the situation in hand and of checking your level of stress.

Another mental technique which is useful in coping with unavoidable stress is self-hypnosis or auto-suggestion. Although many people's skepticism and negative attitudes obliterate its benefits, the technique is effective. Properly used, self-hypnosis is an alteration of consciousness which allows us to relax more easily, and which allows for various self-suggestions to be made.

DEALING WITH THE INEVITABLES

Try this aid to coping. Sit comfortably in a chair. Pick some distant object and focus your attention on it. As you give all of your attention to the object, silently tell yourself that your eyelids are getting heavier and heavier, and that pretty soon your eyelids will close and you'll be very relaxed. This suggestion should be repeated silently every sixty seconds. When your eyelids want to close, allow them to. Then, slowly take a deep breath and hold it for ten seconds. Exhale. Breathe normally and say the word "relax" each time you exhale.

Take another deep breath, hold it, then exhale as you say the word "deeper." As you go further into this state of altered consciousness, repeat the word "deeper" with each exhale. You will feel yourself losing touch with your physical surroundings. (Note: At any time you can come out of this light trance by saying "I'm coming out.")

When you reach a point of great relaxation, give yourself several suggestions—or just one on which to concentrate. Phrase them in a positive manner. Examples: "I am going to feel more relaxed in my next job interview"; "I will not be upset by the meeting tomorrow"; "I will be relaxed at the presentation"; "I will not let my mother-in-law upset me."

When you want to emerge from the light trance do so gently. You might tell yourself that when you get to the count of six, eight, or ten, your eyes will open.

Aside from the addition of the self-suggestion, the method is similar to most relaxation methods. In short, it is up to you to choose the method with which you feel most comfortable.

Stress can be managed. The key to overcoming the negative effects of stress is in knowing everything possible about the stressors of our life, knowing how we react both physically and emotionally to those stressors, and devising methods that deal effectively with those stressors. For most women, harnessing the energy consumed by stressors is a welcome change in life. Once you are in control of your stressors, you will find that every situation has its solution.

The Mastering Stress Program in the following chapter formally teaches you to deal with stress.

The Mastering Stress Program

8. Week One: Getting to Know You

The Mastering Stress Program combines techniques that help you deal with specific as well as long-term stress situations. Underlying the program is the belief that as you come to know more about your particular stressors and your responses to stress you will use this knowledge to manage stress rather than allowing stress to manage you.

Beginning now, and for the next four weeks, you will keep a record of each incident or situation which makes you feel stressed. Use the Stress Incidents Record to keep your account on a daily basis. Jot down each stress incident, then indicate how your body responded—tensing up, constricting throat muscles, grinding teeth, aches, pains, blood pounding, heart racing, diarrhea, nausea, vomiting, or any other physical responses. In a separate column, write down how you felt in the situation—helpless, threatened, out of control, in control, fearful, angry, or whatever emotion best describes your feelings. Write down only comments which will remind you how you handled the situation. Do this for a week, then deal with stress by actively applying the practices which follow.

STRESS INCIDENTS RECORD
WEEK #1

Day	Incident	Physical Response	Emotional Response	Comment
1				
2				
3				
4				

WEEK ONE: GETTING TO KNOW YOU

5 _____

6 _____

7 _____

Additional comments on the week:

Also in this first week, begin to gain a firm idea of how much time you spend in both stress-filled and stress-free activity. Start thinking about how your time may be put to better use. For this first week, record your activities daily on the Time Management Charts which appear at the end of this chapter. Estimate as closely as possible your time spent in each activity. Comment on what you've discovered about how you really spend your time and the effect which analyzing time expenditure has had on your activities. Record information at the end of each day, or early the following morning, so that everything is fresh in your memory.

Now, it is time to determine your Personal Stress Profile (PSP). This profile is made up of your scores on the Compustress form, the Stress Personality Pattern Evaluation (SPPE), the Bodily Stress Indicator, and the Psychological Stress Indicator.

As you complete each of the tests that follow, mark down your score in the PSP on p. 169. If you have already taken some of the tests, skip to the next one — but remember to write down your score in the PSP.

COMPUSTRESS

Instructions: Check those events which have occurred in the last year and those situations which are characteristic of your behavior or experience in the past year.

____ 1. Experienced difficulty sleeping at night
____ 2. Felt nervous or restless
____ 3. Experienced a serious illness
____ 4. Someone close to you experienced a serious illness
____ 5. Suffered the death of someone close
____ 6. Felt grouchy and tense

WEEK ONE: GETTING TO KNOW YOU

___ 7. Drank, smoked or ate more than you feel was good for you
___ 8. Experienced financial problems
___ 9. Changed jobs
___ 10. Lost your job
___ 11. Got married
___ 12. Reconciled with your spouse
___ 13. Got divorced
___ 14. Separated from your spouse
___ 15. Broke off a meaningful romantic relationship
___ 16. Experienced an unwanted pregnancy
___ 17. Experienced a desired pregnancy
___ 18. Had an abortion — either spontaneous or induced
___ 19. Experienced dissatisfaction with your physical appearance
___ 20. Experienced dissatisfaction with your professional achievements
___ 21. Were a crime victim
___ 22. Felt overwhelmed by responsibilities
___ 23. Felt you had no time for yourself
___ 24. Were absent minded more often than not
___ 25. Experienced an increase in personal responsibilities

WEEK ONE: GETTING TO KNOW YOU

____ 26. Experienced an increase in professional responsibilities
____ 27. Experienced a serious accident
____ 28. Experienced dissatisfaction with your sex life
____ 29. Experienced difficulty concentrating on your work
____ 30. Felt unloved by your family
____ 31. Argued seriously with a family member
____ 32. Felt socially "out of it"
____ 33. Moved from one residence to another
____ 34. Found yourself relying on alcohol, tranquilizers, or other crutches
____ 35. Discovered your husband or lover was cheating
____ 36. Began an affair
____ 37. Added a member to your household
____ 38. Lost weight without explanation
____ 39. Experienced a business loss, the loss of an investment, or a heavy increase in financial responsibilities
____ 40. Felt that life was meaningless

If your Compustress score is from 1 to 10, you are in LOW range; 11 to 25, MODERATE; 26 to 40, HIGH.

WEEK ONE: GETTING TO KNOW YOU

Now identify your particular stress pattern by responding to the stress personality pattern evaluation (SPPE) which follows. Record this score on the PSP. If your SPPE score falls between 20 and 25, you are in the LOW range; 26 to 40, MODERATE; 41 and above, HIGH.

STRESS PERSONALITY PATTERN EVALUATION

Read each question carefully and fill in the corresponding blank, rating how accurately you feel the question describes you. If you feel that it is *not at all* relevant to your personality, place a 1 in the blank. If it is *somewhat* relevant, then place a 2 in the blank. If the item is *typical* of your personality, then place a 3 in the blank.

1 — not at all   2 — somewhat   3 — typically

_____ 1. Do you move, walk and eat rapidly?
_____ 2. Are you impatient with the pace of the world?
_____ 3. Do you frequently do two or more things at once?
_____ 4. Do you often become involved in several projects at the same time?

WEEK ONE: GETTING TO KNOW YOU

____ 5. Does relaxing and doing absolutely nothing for several hours make you feel guilty?

____ 6. Do you become irritated out of proportion with others' slowness?

____ 7. Do you have a habit of looking at your watch or clock often?

____ 8. Do you emphasize strongly various key words in your speech, even when no real need for this exists?

____ 9. Do you hurry your sentences along, finishing the last few words as quickly as possible?

____ 10. Are you preoccupied with your own thoughts?

____ 11. Are you preoccupied with acquiring material possessions?

____ 12. Do you feel a chronic sense of having too little time?

____ 13. Do you have any characteristic gestures or nervous tics?

____ 14. Do you feel the need to handle every problem alone?

____ 15. Do you feel that part of your success is due to your ability to do things faster than others?

____ 16. Are you preoccupied with evaluating your performance and that of others in terms of productivity?

____ 17. Do you have little time for hobbies or nonproductive (in terms of money) activities?

____ 18. Are you referred to by others as being "hard-driving"?

____ 19. When you meet another Type A personality, do you feel little compassion for her affliction?

____ 20. When you meet another Type A personality, do you feel the need to challenge her?

How do you respond to stress? To determine this, fill in your responses to the pressure points checklist, and also record this score on the PSP.

PRESSURE POINTS CHECKLIST

Instructions: Read over each item on this list of characteristic responses of individuals under stress and place an X next to those signs which describe your stress response(s).

____ 1. Pain in the neck or the lower back
____ 2. Frequent need to urinate

WEEK ONE: GETTING TO KNOW YOU

____ 3. Excessive perspiring
____ 4. Insomnia
____ 5. Desire to strike out at others
____ 6. Inability to relax
____ 7. Pounding of the heart
____ 8. Feeling of blood rushing to your head
____ 9. Inability to concentrate
____ 10. Headaches which last more than an hour
____ 11. Nervous laughter or giggling
____ 12. Heavy smoking
____ 13. Feeling of disorientation
____ 14. Undefinable fears and anxiety
____ 15. Dryness of the mouth and the throat
____ 16. Lack of appetite
____ 17. Compulsive eating
____ 18. Diarrhea
____ 19. Indigestion
____ 20. Queasiness in the stomach
____ 21. Vomiting
____ 22. Stuttering
____ 23. Nervous tics
____ 24. Uncontrollable urge to cry
____ 25. Emotional tenseness
____ 26. Increased smoking
____ 27. Increased intake of alcohol
____ 28. Increased use of prescription drugs

WEEK ONE: GETTING TO KNOW YOU

_____ 29. Frequent accidents
_____ 30. Nightmares
_____ 31. Grinding of teeth
_____ 32. Pre-menstrual tension
_____ 33. Missed menstrual cycle
_____ 34. Impulsive behavior
_____ 35. Fatigue
_____ 36. Trembling
_____ 37. Frequent loss of temper
_____ 38. Acting edgy and keyed up
_____ 39. Vertigo
_____ 40. Desire to avoid others
_____ 41. Depression
_____ 42. Tendency to be upset by unexpected sounds
_____ 43. Anxiety based on no specific cause
_____ 44. Skin irritation

There are two more checklists to complete so that a total picture of your stress reactions and patterns can emerge. For each list, count the number of items checked and record that number on the PSP. You should be aware of the extent to which you are stressed and just how far you have gone beyond your personal stress threshold.

WEEK ONE: GETTING TO KNOW YOU

BODILY STRESS INDICATOR

Instructions: Check off those items which describe you and your physical stress symptoms.

____ 1. Persistent feeling of fatigue
____ 2. Inhibited ability to cry
____ 3. Chronic heartburn
____ 4. Tendency to faint or to feel nauseous
____ 5. Compulsive eating when anxious
____ 6. Obesity
____ 7. Persistent inability to experience orgasm
____ 8. Nervous energy which makes you fidget
____ 9. High blood pressure
____ 10. Insomnia
____ 11. Involuntary tightening of the muscles
____ 12. Chronic constipation
____ 13. Chronic diarrhea
____ 14. Chronic bloated feeling
____ 15. Chronic headache
____ 16. Tendency to cry easily
____ 17. Breathlessness

WEEK ONE: GETTING TO KNOW YOU

PSYCHOLOGICAL STRESS INDICATOR

Instructions: Check off those items which describe you and your stress symptoms.

____ 1. Feelings of inadequacy in parenting
____ 2. Underlying hostility
____ 3. Fear of being alone
____ 4. Somber outlook on life
____ 5. Lack of a sense of humor
____ 6. Compulsive fear of diseases such as cancer and heart disease
____ 7. Lack of desire to relax or take a vacation
____ 8. Money worries
____ 9. Feelings of rejection by family or friends
____ 10. Inordinate fear of heights, close spaces and natural disasters
____ 11. Chronic feeling of inability to cope with life
____ 12. Feelings of isolation
____ 13. Constant anxiety regarding death
____ 14. Lack of powers of concentration
____ 15. Chronic boredom
____ 16. Desire to "chuck it all" and disappear

WEEK ONE: GETTING TO KNOW YOU

_____ 17. Feelings of social inadequacy
_____ 18. Despair regarding holidays

PERSONAL STRESS PROFILE

COMPUSTRESS
Score: _____ Low, Moderate or High (Circle One).

STRESS PERSONALITY PATTERN EVALUATION
Score: _____ Low, Moderate or High (Circle One).

PRESSURE POINTS CHECKLIST
  Score: _____

BODILY STRESS INDICATOR
  Score: _____

PSYCHOLOGICAL STRESS INDICATOR
  Score: _____

Let's take a look at those scores. As you might recall from the earlier discussion, a LOW score on the Compustress measure shows that you are handling stress well in your life. A MODERATE score indicates emerging health problems and a need for a re-patterning in specific areas of your life. If the score is HIGH, it is mandatory that you learn to manage stress because it is threatening your well-being.

WEEK ONE: GETTING TO KNOW YOU

What is your Stress Personality Pattern Evaluation score? If you're at the LOW end, you have no stress problem whatsoever. In the MODERATE range, you appear to have a substantial amount of control over your stressors and, with attention to diet and activity, the balance should remain. If you are in the 40-and-above category (HIGH), then stress has really begun to wreak havoc with your life, especially if your score is from the middle to high end of the scale (maximum of 60). Your physiological and psychological well-being are in danger and you are a serious candidate for stress-related ills.

Now look again at your Stress Personality Pattern Evaluation score and that of the Compustress. Are both scores in the HIGH category? If so, then you are risking your health with each day that you continue your present pattern of behavior. Even if you are in the MODERATE, or acceptable range, you are bordering on danger unless you take strict control of your life and stressors.

Let's move down to the Pressure Points Checklist. Take a close look at the pressure points that you checked. A few are relatively easy to handle, but too many pressure points can be harmful to your bodily and psychologi-

WEEK ONE: GETTING TO KNOW YOU

cal health. Given the serious nature of some of the pressure points, you should be concerned if four or more are checked off. Many of the reactions show that your body is not handling stress in a productive manner.

The final measures are the Bodily Stress Indicator and the Psychological Stress Indicator. Did you check off only one symptom on the Bodily Stress Indicator? Two? Three? Four? Five? Six? More than six? Did you check off only one symptom on the Psychological Stress Indicator? Two? Three? Four? Five? Six? More than six?

If you checked off more than two of the bodily stress indicators that's evidence that your present life style is placing your body under high risk of illness or disease due to excessive stress. If you checked off more than four of the psychological symptoms, excessive stress has made you a high-risk candidate. You *must* work to change your way of dealing with stress.

The goal of Week One is to make you aware of the damaging effect that stress has on your life and to identify aspects of your life which are particularly affected. In Week Two, you will learn more about your particular stressors and begin to develop long-term strategies to-

WEEK ONE: GETTING TO KNOW YOU

ward handling the stress in your life.

For this first week, keep both your Stress Incidents Record and Time Management Chart on a daily basis. Remember in filling out the time management charts that the TOTAL STRESSFUL HOURS and the TOTAL STRESS-FREE HOURS do not have to add up to twenty-four hours. Be as detailed as you can in recording items. The observations you make are vital to understanding your particular stressors and stress responses. Once the enemy is identified, then the process of managing can begin.

WEEK ONE: GETTING TO KNOW YOU

TIME MANAGEMENT CHART
WEEK #1   DAY: _____

Time Spent

- ____ 1. Sleeping
- ____ 2. Eating
- ____ 3. Working at your job (include work taken home and business lunches)
- ____ 4. Relaxing and doing *nothing* else
- ____ 5. Taking care of yourself (include dressing, putting on makeup, showering and exercising)
- ____ 6. Housekeeping (include meal preparation)
- ____ 7. Taking care of children
- ____ 8. Spending time with your husband/boyfriend
- ____ 9. Entertaining yourself (include reading, watching television, listening to music, and any hobbies)
- ____ 10. Shopping
- ____ 11. Traveling (include commuting time)
- ____ 12. Socializing with friends
- ____ 13. Other (specify)_____
- ____ **TOTAL STRESSFUL HOURS**
- ____ **TOTAL STRESS-FREE HOURS**

WEEK ONE: GETTING TO KNOW YOU

TIME MANAGEMENT CHART

WEEK #1   DAY: _____

Time Spent

____ 1. Sleeping
____ 2. Eating
____ 3. Working at your job (include work taken home and business lunches)
____ 4. Relaxing and doing *nothing* else
____ 5. Taking care of yourself (include dressing, putting on makeup, showering and exercising)
____ 6. Housekeeping (include meal preparation)
____ 7. Taking care of children
____ 8. Spending time with your husband/boyfriend
____ 9. Entertaining yourself (include reading, watching television, listening to music, and any hobbies)
____ 10. Shopping
____ 11. Traveling (include commuting time)
____ 12. Socializing with friends
____ 13. Other (specify)_____
____ TOTAL STRESSFUL HOURS
____ TOTAL STRESS-FREE HOURS

WEEK ONE: GETTING TO KNOW YOU

TIME MANAGEMENT CHART

WEEK #1   DAY: _____

Time Spent

____ 1. Sleeping
____ 2. Eating
____ 3. Working at your job (include work taken home and business lunches)
____ 4. Relaxing and doing *nothing* else
____ 5. Taking care of yourself (include dressing, putting on makeup, showering and exercising)
____ 6. Housekeeping (include meal preparation)
____ 7. Taking care of children
____ 8. Spending time with your husband/boyfriend
____ 9. Entertaining yourself (include reading, watching television, listening to music, and any hobbies)
____ 10. Shopping
____ 11. Traveling (include commuting time)
____ 12. Socializing with friends
____ 13. Other (specify)_____
____ TOTAL STRESSFUL HOURS
____ TOTAL STRESS-FREE HOURS

WEEK ONE: GETTING TO KNOW YOU

TIME MANAGEMENT CHART

WEEK #1   **DAY:** _____

Time Spent

____ 1. Sleeping
____ 2. Eating
____ 3. Working at your job (include work taken home and business lunches)
____ 4. Relaxing and doing *nothing* else
____ 5. Taking care of yourself (include dressing, putting on makeup, showering and exercising)
____ 6. Housekeeping (include meal preparation)
____ 7. Taking care of children
____ 8. Spending time with your husband/boyfriend
____ 9. Entertaining yourself (include reading, watching television, listening to music, and any hobbies)
____ 10. Shopping
____ 11. Traveling (include commuting time)
____ 12. Socializing with friends
____ 13. Other (specify)_____
____ TOTAL STRESSFUL HOURS
____ TOTAL STRESS-FREE HOURS

WEEK ONE: GETTING TO KNOW YOU

TIME MANAGEMENT CHART

WEEK #1   **DAY:** _____

Time Spent

____ 1. Sleeping
____ 2. Eating
____ 3. Working at your job (include work taken home and business lunches)
____ 4. Relaxing and doing *nothing* else
____ 5. Taking care of yourself (include dressing, putting on makeup, showering and exercising)
____ 6. Housekeeping (include meal preparation)
____ 7. Taking care of children
____ 8. Spending time with your husband/boyfriend
____ 9. Entertaining yourself (include reading, watching television, listening to music, and any hobbies)
____ 10. Shopping
____ 11. Traveling (include commuting time)
____ 12. Socializing with friends
____ 13. Other (specify)_____
____ TOTAL STRESSFUL HOURS
____ TOTAL STRESS-FREE HOURS

WEEK ONE: GETTING TO KNOW YOU

TIME MANAGEMENT CHART
WEEK #1   DAY: _____

Time Spent

_____ 1. Sleeping
_____ 2. Eating
_____ 3. Working at your job (include work taken home and business lunches)
_____ 4. Relaxing and doing *nothing* else
_____ 5. Taking care of yourself (include dressing, putting on makeup, showering and exercising)
_____ 6. Housekeeping (include meal preparation)
_____ 7. Taking care of children
_____ 8. Spending time with your husband/boyfriend
_____ 9. Entertaining yourself (include reading, watching television, listening to music, and any hobbies)
_____ 10. Shopping
_____ 11. Traveling (include commuting time)
_____ 12. Socializing with friends
_____ 13. Other (specify)_____
_____ TOTAL STRESSFUL HOURS
_____ TOTAL STRESS-FREE HOURS

WEEK ONE: GETTING TO KNOW YOU

TIME MANAGEMENT CHART

WEEK #1   DAY: _____

Time Spent

____ 1. Sleeping
____ 2. Eating
____ 3. Working at your job (include work taken home and business lunches)
____ 4. Relaxing and doing *nothing* else
____ 5. Taking care of yourself (include dressing, putting on makeup, showering and exercising)
____ 6. Housekeeping (include meal preparation)
____ 7. Taking care of children
____ 8. Spending time with your husband/boyfriend
____ 9. Entertaining yourself (include reading, watching television, listening to music, and any hobbies)
____ 10. Shopping
____ 11. Traveling (include commuting time)
____ 12. Socializing with friends
____ 13. Other (specify)_____
____ **TOTAL STRESSFUL HOURS**
____ **TOTAL STRESS-FREE HOURS**

9. Week Two: Learning to Cope

Let's start off the second week of the Mastering Stress Program by reviewing your entries in the Stress Incidents Record for Week One. What are the stressors that result in stress responses in your life? Children? Work? Parents? Bills? Mechanical objects?

How are you dealing physically with your stress? Are you grinding your teeth? Perspiring? Feeling nauseous? Drinking heavily? Smoking more?

What are your emotional reactions to stress? Are you angered? Fearful? Feeling out of control?

From a review of the stress situations encountered in a week, you have probably found

WEEK TWO: LEARNING TO COPE

that it is more life's little annoyances that stimulate the stress response in you. It's time to begin dealing with those little annoyances.

You also may see that your responses to stressors follow a definite pattern. Perhaps you run for the coffee pot, or begin to eat compulsively. Maybe you begin to feel your stomach contract, your back stiffen. Learn all that you can about your responses in order to create better methods for managing your stress.

If you eat properly, and limit your intake of alcohol, caffeine, nicotine and sugar, you will find that your ability to withstand stress (your stress threshold) will increase dramatically. The little stressors are more tolerable when our bodies are in good condition and we feel a general sense of well-being. For this to happen, repatterning must occur.

In essence, you must take control of your life and work out a schedule which will not only allow you to accomplish what is necessary but which also allows you to *relax*. Try to stand at a distance from the stress-producing situation and tell yourself that it is *only temporary*. At the same time, analyze what it is in the situation that results in a stress reaction (stressors) and how you are handling the stressors (your stress response). Approach situations as you do in recording stress incidents in the Stress Incidents Record.

Now review your Time Management Charts for the first week. What is your average time spent relaxing? Is more of the day spent in stressful situations than in non-stressful time? Are you working more than socializing? Is eating time relegated to only minute portions of the day? Look at your schedule and evaluate where you might be able to decrease some of the stress.

Are you happy with what you see as your week's activities? Take a close look at each category. Are there areas in which you would want to spend more time daily? Less time? Fill in the chart below and set goals for the way in which you wish to manage your time, rather than having your time managed for you!

TIME MANAGEMENT GOAL

Column A = Current Daily Average*
Column B = Desired Daily Average

A	B	
___	___	1. Sleeping
___	___	2. Eating
___	___	3. Working at your job (include work taken home and busi-

WEEK TWO: LEARNING TO COPE

___ ___		ness lunches)
___ ___	4.	Relaxing and doing *nothing* else
___ ___	5.	Taking care of yourself (include dressing, putting on makeup, showering and exercising)
___ ___	6.	Housekeeping (include meal preparation)
___ ___	7.	Taking care of children
___ ___	8.	Spending time with your husband/boyfriend
___ ___	9.	Entertaining yourself (include reading, watching television, listening to music, and any hobbies)
___ ___	10.	Shopping
___ ___	11.	Traveling (include commuting time)
___ ___	12.	Socializing with friends
___ ___	13.	Other (Specify)_____
___ ___		TOTAL STRESSFUL HOURS
___ ___		TOTAL STRESS-FREE HOURS

*To obtain this figure, add your figures for each category for the week and divide by seven.

WEEK TWO: LEARNING TO COPE

You can meet those goals, and reduce the negative effects of stress on your life, by re-patterning your life. In the process, you will learn to make stress a productive rather than destructive force. You will learn these re-patterning techniques and long-term coping strategies in Week Three of the Mastering Stress Program. For now, there are several ways to deal with your stressors on a short-term basis which will lessen the destructive effects of stress on your body and mind.

When you feel especially stressed, use the two short-term techniques that you learned earlier in this book: deep breathing and muscle relaxation.

DEEP BREATHING EXERCISE

This brief exercise will prove helpful in relieving some of the tension which stress can create. Sit back in your chair. Breathe in deeply through your nose (mouth closed). Then exhale deeply through the mouth, emptying the lungs totally. Do this five times. Feel the tension leave your body as you force all the air out of your lungs.

WEEK TWO: LEARNING TO COPE

MUSCLE RELAXATION EXERCISE

Lie down on a carpeted surface. Begin to tense every part of your body, one portion at a time, following the instructions below. You may have soothing music playing in the background.

Tighten up the muscles of your toes. Now your ankles. Keep these muscles tense as you tighten the muscles in your calves. Feel the effort in maintaining the tenseness. Hold the muscles tense and tighten your knees, then your thighs. Tighten your buttocks muscles. Feel the muscles straining. Tighten your stomach muscles. Now the rib cage. Tense your shoulders. Tighten your finger muscles. Now your arms. Tighten the muscles in your neck. Squint and feel the muscles of your face tighten. Hold the muscles tensed for a full minute.

Now relax those muscles, one muscle at a time. The muscles tensed last will be relaxed first.

Relax the muscles of the forehead. Allow the muscles in your cheeks to go slack and stop squinting. Now relax your neck. Feel the relief as your shoulders slowly fall downward and let the muscles of your arms and fingers untense.

WEEK TWO: LEARNING TO COPE

Let your stomach muscles loosen. Loosen the muscles of your rib cage. Your buttocks muscles must be straining. Let them relax. Now to your legs, the only parts of your body which should now be tight. Become aware of how they feel, tensed and waiting to be relaxed. Relax your thighs. Let the tightness leave your knees. Feel the calves slowly loosen in relief. Now the ankles. Then your feet and toes.

The muscles in your body should now be relaxed. No tightness in the neck. No stiffness in the shoulders. Keep your eyes closed. Remember to inhale deeply through your nose. Exhale deeply through your mouth (empty your lungs).

Tense those muscles as hard as you can.

You are trying to squeeze the stress out of your muscles and out of your body.

If stress has made sleeping difficult for you as the tensions of the day continue to plague you far into the night, do the Muscle Relaxation Exercise before bedtime. The tension will flow out from your body and the resulting tranquility will let you float off to sleep.

In addition, you will find the following coping strategies invaluable whenever stressors have made your muscles tight and stiff or when you are feeling overwrought.

COPING STRATEGIES

1. Walk
2. Exercise
3. Massage those tight muscles in the neck, back, shoulders and other areas of the body
4. Stretch, either standing up or sitting down
5. Breathe deeply, at least ten or twelve times
6. Do the Muscle Relaxation Exercise or Deep Breathing Exercise
7. Take a hot bath—if the circumstances permit
8. Talk to someone—or talk to yourself
9. Retreat from the stressor for a while

Continue to record stress incidents in the Stress Incidents Record for the coming week. Remain aware of your stressors and of your stress responses. Most of all, use the relaxation exercises and coping strategies to relieve periods of stress whenever possible.

STRESS INCIDENTS RECORD
WEEK #2

Day	Incident	Physical Response	Emotional Response	Comment
1				
2				
3				
4				
5				
6				
7				

Additional comments on the week:

WEEK TWO: LEARNING TO COPE

You should also continue to keep a record of how you spend your time so that you can come closer to achieving your time management goals.

WEEK TWO: LEARNING TO COPE

TIME MANAGEMENT CHART

WEEK #2　　　　　DAY: _____

Time Spent

____ 1. Sleeping
____ 2. Eating
____ 3. Working at your job (include work taken home and business lunches)
____ 4. Relaxing and doing *nothing* else
____ 5. Taking care of yourself (include dressing, putting on makeup, showering and exercising)
____ 6. Housekeeping (include meal preparation)
____ 7. Taking care of children
____ 8. Spending time with your husband/boyfriend
____ 9. Entertaining yourself (include reading, watching television, listening to music, and any hobbies)
____ 10. Shopping
____ 11. Traveling (include commuting time)
____ 12. Socializing with friends
____ 13. Other (specify)_____
____ TOTAL STRESSFUL HOURS
____ TOTAL STRESS-FREE HOURS

WEEK TWO: LEARNING TO COPE

TIME MANAGEMENT CHART

WEEK #2　　　　DAY: _____

Time Spent

____　1. Sleeping
____　2. Eating
____　3. Working at your job (include work taken home and business lunches)
____　4. Relaxing and doing *nothing* else
____　5. Taking care of yourself (include dressing, putting on makeup, showering and exercising)
____　6. Housekeeping (include meal preparation)
____　7. Taking care of children
____　8. Spending time with your husband/boyfriend
____　9. Entertaining yourself (include reading, watching television, listening to music, and any hobbies)
____ 10. Shopping
____ 11. Traveling (include commuting time)
____ 12. Socializing with friends
____ 13. Other (specify)_____
____ TOTAL STRESSFUL HOURS
____ TOTAL STRESS-FREE HOURS

WEEK TWO: LEARNING TO COPE

TIME MANAGEMENT CHART

WEEK #2   DAY: _____

Time Spent

_____ 1. Sleeping
_____ 2. Eating
_____ 3. Working at your job (include work taken home and business lunches)
_____ 4. Relaxing and doing *nothing* else
_____ 5. Taking care of yourself (include dressing, putting on makeup, showering and exercising)
_____ 6. Housekeeping (include meal preparation)
_____ 7. Taking care of children
_____ 8. Spending time with your husband/boyfriend
_____ 9. Entertaining yourself (include reading, watching television, listening to music, and any hobbies)
_____ 10. Shopping
_____ 11. Traveling (include commuting time)
_____ 12. Socializing with friends
_____ 13. Other (specify)_____
_____ TOTAL STRESSFUL HOURS
_____ TOTAL STRESS-FREE HOURS

TIME MANAGEMENT CHART

WEEK #2　　　　　DAY: _____

Time Spent

_____ 1. Sleeping
_____ 2. Eating
_____ 3. Working at your job (include work taken home and business lunches)
_____ 4. Relaxing and doing *nothing* else
_____ 5. Taking care of yourself (include dressing, putting on makeup, showering and exercising)
_____ 6. Housekeeping (include meal preparation)
_____ 7. Taking care of children
_____ 8. Spending time with your husband/boyfriend
_____ 9. Entertaining yourself (include reading, watching television, listening to music, and any hobbies)
_____ 10. Shopping
_____ 11. Traveling (include commuting time)
_____ 12. Socializing with friends
_____ 13. Other (specify)_____
_____ TOTAL STRESSFUL HOURS
_____ TOTAL STRESS-FREE HOURS

WEEK TWO: LEARNING TO COPE

TIME MANAGEMENT CHART

WEEK #2 · DAY: _____

Time Spent

_____ 1. Sleeping
_____ 2. Eating
_____ 3. Working at your job (include work taken home and business lunches)
_____ 4. Relaxing and doing *nothing* else
_____ 5. Taking care of yourself (include dressing, putting on makeup, showering and exercising)
_____ 6. Housekeeping (include meal preparation)
_____ 7. Taking care of children
_____ 8. Spending time with your husband/boyfriend
_____ 9. Entertaining yourself (include reading, watching television, listening to music, and any hobbies)
_____ 10. Shopping
_____ 11. Traveling (include commuting time)
_____ 12. Socializing with friends
_____ 13. Other (specify)_____
_____ **TOTAL STRESSFUL HOURS**
_____ **TOTAL STRESS-FREE HOURS**

WEEK TWO: LEARNING TO COPE

TIME MANAGEMENT CHART

WEEK #2   **DAY:** _____

Time Spent

____ 1. Sleeping
____ 2. Eating
____ 3. Working at your job (include work taken home and business lunches)
____ 4. Relaxing and doing *nothing* else
____ 5. Taking care of yourself (include dressing, putting on makeup, showering and exercising)
____ 6. Housekeeping (include meal preparation)
____ 7. Taking care of children
____ 8. Spending time with your husband/boyfriend
____ 9. Entertaining yourself (include reading, watching television, listening to music, and any hobbies)
____ 10. Shopping
____ 11. Traveling (include commuting time)
____ 12. Socializing with friends
____ 13. Other (specify)_____
____ **TOTAL STRESSFUL HOURS**
____ **TOTAL STRESS-FREE HOURS**

WEEK TWO: LEARNING TO COPE

TIME MANAGEMENT CHART

WEEK #2   DAY: _____

Time Spent

____ 1. Sleeping
____ 2. Eating
____ 3. Working at your job (include work taken home and business lunches)
____ 4. Relaxing and doing *nothing* else
____ 5. Taking care of yourself (include dressing, putting on makeup, showering and exercising)
____ 6. Housekeeping (include meal preparation)
____ 7. Taking care of children
____ 8. Spending time with your husband/boyfriend
____ 9. Entertaining yourself (include reading, watching television, listening to music, and any hobbies)
____ 10. Shopping
____ 11. Traveling (include commuting time)
____ 12. Socializing with friends
____ 13. Other (specify)_____
____ TOTAL STRESSFUL HOURS
____ TOTAL STRESS-FREE HOURS

10. Week Three: Learning to Manage Stress

In the last two weeks, as well as throughout your reading of the early chapters of this book, you have been re-educating yourself regarding stress and your stress symptoms and responses. You have been gradually learning the extent to which stress has successfully managed you for too long. Your behavior, your thoughts, your habits and your life have been orchestrated by stressors. These stressors result in a stress response that has often undesirable effects on your health, your personal relationships and your professional performance.

Through recording your stress incidents, you have been alerted to the types and varieties of stressors which operate in your life. You know how you react physically and emotionally. You know what symptoms you suffer from as a result of unmanaged stress in your life. In addition, you should now be aware of the means you employ to cope with stress situations.

Look at the Stress Incidents Record. Examine how your stress history has changed in two weeks. Look at the number of stress situations recorded in the first week. How many were there? How many stress situations did you record in the last week?

Has there been an increase in the number of stress situations recorded from the first to second weeks or a decrease?

Look at the columns listing your physical and emotional reactions to stressors. What type of change has occurred? Are your reactions different? Are they more intense? Less intense? If they are less intense, this may very well be the result of your increased awareness of the effects of stress on your life.

What about your attempts to cope with stress situations? What has changed in this area? Would you describe your reactions in the second week as being among those negative reactions which we discussed in the second week of the program? Do you feel that you are coping negatively in most instances? Positively?

Your negative reactions are going to be eliminated as you assume mastery over stress. You have

WEEK THREE: LEARNING TO MANAGE STRESS

taken the first important steps toward this mastery by examining what stress is and how you are specifically affected by stress.

It is now time to begin re-patterning your life, utilizing specific techniques in order to conquer stress.

It is important for your long-range well-being that you have an overall plan of action which will condition your body and mind to deal effectively and productively with stress in your life in total — not just at isolated points of stress.

From your self-analysis, accomplished through an examination of the tests and record-keeping, you now know what causes you stress, your specific symptoms of stress, and your favored coping techniques. Because your chosen techniques have been ineffective, you must develop a plan of action that will work for you. Ideally, you will develop a wide range of coping techniques and use them as needed. Stress can only be successfully handled if we master the basic techniques of psychological survival, and if we have the imagination and flexibility to use them appropriately.

You certainly can't avoid stress — that's something that this book has emphasized. Rather than avoid all situations which might be stressful, you must learn how to live and to behave in a way which will prepare you for them. When you know that certain stressors will continue to exist, then you can prepare for the next confrontation. Even unexpected stress can become manageable if you remain ready by keeping mentally and physically healthy, by clarifying your goals and values, and by maintaining a high sense of self-esteem.

Several preventive techniques exist which provide a valuable, if general, rule-of-thumb toward eliminating many stressors from our lives. At first, you might feel the techniques are too matter-of-fact to help you deal with the complex tensions which often engulf you. It is *because* they are so matter-of-fact that they provide a means of successfully re-patterning—but not revolutionizing—your life

PREVENTIVE TECHNIQUES

1. Accept yourself
2. Cultivate a trusted friend or two to share your confidences
3. Act in a constructive manner to eliminate sources of stress
4. Vary your acquaintances
5. Vary your activities
6. Use the scientific management method of problem-solving to regulate your life
   (1) Identify your problem (stressor)
   (2) Devise several solutions
   (3) Analyze the alternatives

WEEK THREE: LEARNING TO MANAGE STRESS

    (4) Make a decision based on the analysis
7. Maintain good physical health by paying attention to nutrition and exercise

STRESS MANAGEMENT EXERCISE

You must also have a plan of action to confront stressors. Let's look at an extreme example of the way in which you might find being prepared for stress valuable. In the first chapter of this book, you were asked to imagine a scene in which you felt physically threatened. The idea was to describe the way in which your body reacted, and how you felt — tense, fearful, nauseous, etc. Even that scene, which many of us might encounter in one way or another, while running out to the store at night, going to a meeting or a class, or just having darkness fall sooner than we expect, offers several alternatives for management.

Let's recall, once again, the image. Imagine that it is a warm spring or summer evening. The air is sweet-smelling and there is a cool breeze blowing softly against your skin. You are out for a walk down a familiar street in a familiar neighborhood. You are walking peacefully along, alone, and letting your mind roam tranquilly. *Allow your mind to build up an image of serenity*. There is no one around and you are glad for the solitude.

WEEK THREE: LEARNING TO MANAGE STRESS

You walk along for a few minutes, enjoying yourself and being lulled into a feeling of complacency. Suddenly behind you comes the sound of footsteps. You look around but see no one. Then bushes quiver off the walk behind you. You walk on and hear the sound of twigs being trampled on. You walk faster and the sounds come faster and appear to be closer.

Allow your body to react as if this were really happening to you. Experience, for the moment, the fear of apprehension, of being stalked on a deserted street which appeared friendly but which is now menacing.

You are having a stress reaction. How can you cope? Let's analyze the situation rationally.

What is your primary stressor in this situation?

_____

_____

_____

_____

_____ .

What might be other, less obvious stressors?

_____

_____

WEEK THREE: LEARNING TO MANAGE STRESS

_____
_____
_____ .

These, too, are stressors although they may be internalized reactions or more personal bases for stress responses.

In this situation, there appears to be little time to examine whether or not a tried and true method for dealing with stress exists, or what it is doing at the moment to your body and mind. However, you still must determine the best way, *in this situation,* to deal with the stressor(s).

Will your reaction be *fight, flight* or *tolerance?*

What are the pitfalls of each of these reactions, in the absence of further information? If you choose to fight, what can occur? What of retreat in this situation?

Of course, tolerating the stressor and continuing on your way may result in increased stress, if your body and mind are suffering anxiety to any degree. This is one situation in which such coping techniques (which you would utilize until the stress passes in less physically threatening circumstances) as the relaxation response technique, muscle relaxation, and massage would be inappropriate. To clear your senses, you should, however, breathe deeply and keep walking to alleviate some of the stress. This will enable you to rapidly utilize the method suggested earlier under Preventive Techniques:

1. Identify your problem (stressors)
2. Devise several solutions (fight, flight, or retreat)
3. Analyze the alternatives (your chances of successfully terminating the stress, in this case)
4. Make a decision based on your analysis

Now, note below one or several chosen mean(s) of dealing with this stress situation. What are your alternatives?

_____
_____
_____
_____
_____ .

As you can see from this example, and from your responses, there is no "formula" for dealing with stress. Each of us has to know her own strengths and weaknesses. Certainly, you can repattern your life to assure that you avoid particular and common stress situations. More effective, however, is a *mental* re-patterning regarding your response to stressors. Go through the steps of the Stress Management Checklist which follows. Once you have devised sure-fire plans for dealing with your common stressors, they will cease to take their toll on your mental and physical well-being.

STRESS MANAGEMENT CHECKLIST

1. Identify your specific stressor(s). What is eliciting the stress response?
2. Have you a tried-and-true method for dealing with the specific stressor?
3. What is the stress situation doing, at this moment, to your body? Your mind?
4. What is the best way to deal with the specific stressor?

a. Tolerate it since it will probably do no harm and will eventually disappear?
b. Arm yourself both physically and mentally and fight it?
c. Leave the situation and, thus, the stressor entirely?

Focus on applying this approach to managing stress situations in this third week of the Mastering Stress Program. Watch how quickly formerly in-

WEEK THREE: LEARNING TO MANAGE STRESS

surmountable stressors become manageable. Review the changes in your Stress Incidents Record. You might even find that such stressors may begin to work *for* rather than *against* you!

Don't forget. Continue to practice the Deep Breathing and Muscle Relaxation exercises whenever stress threatens.

STRESS INCIDENTS RECORD
WEEK #3

Day	Incident	Physical Response	Emotional Response	Comment
1				
2				
3				
4				
5				

WEEK THREE: LEARNING TO MANAGE STRESS

6
_____

7
_____

Additional comments on the week:

11. Week Four: Making Stress Work For You

For three weeks now, you have been watching carefully to see just what causes a stress reaction in your life. You may have been surprised to find that specific stressors continue to plague you — and they have done so for a long while. The logical question which you may have asked is, "Why haven't I done something about them?"

Well, until now, you really didn't know that there was anything you could do — except to just grin (more likely grit your teeth) and bear it. In these last three weeks, you have learned a great deal.

By keeping a record of your stress incidents, you have determined which situations are most likely to stress you. Even if you can't avoid such situations entirely, at least now you are ready for them.

Being aware of your common stressors allows you to plan ahead — to either prevent the stressors from arising or to select an appropriate means of dealing with stressors. It is valuable, at this point, to examine the entries on your Stress Incidents Record.

Has increased knowledge regarding stress and its effects on your well-being affected the number of stress situations you experience? Look at your sheets and compare Week One with Week Three. Do you see an increase in the number of stress situations from the first to the third week or a decrease? How have your reactions changed? How many were positive in the first week? Negative? What about the third week? Enter these responses on the Stress Incidents Record Results form which follows and consider if change has occurred.

You have probably learned to cope substantially better with the stressors of life. Nonetheless, there will continue to exist a variety of situations which will trigger the stress response. We will practice handling these trigger situations a little later in this lesson.

STRESS INCIDENTS RECORD RESULTS

WEEK ONE	WEEK THREE
Number of incidents _____	Number of incidents _____
Number of positive reactions _____	Number of positive reactions _____
Number of negative reactions _____	Number of negative reactions _____

For now, it is time to gather some measurable evidence as to how effectively you have learned to manage stress by retaking the Stress Personality Pattern Evaluation. You responded to the form in the first week before learning more thoroughly the ways of stress management. It is now time to respond to the form again and to compare the two scores. Remember, respond to the questions according to the new way in which you feel and to the new patterns which you may have developed in your fight against harmful stress.

STRESS PERSONALITY PATTERN EVALUATION

Instructions: Read each question carefully and fill in the corresponding blank, rating how accurately the question describes you. If you feel that it is *not at all* relevant to your personality, place a 1 in the blank. If it is *somewhat* relevant, then place a 2 in the blank. If the item is *typical* of your personality, then place a 3 in the blank. For instance, if you often rush the last few words of sentences, fill in 3 (typically).

1 — not at all   2 — somewhat   3 — typically

____ 1. Do you move, walk and eat rapidly?

____ 2. Are you impatient with the pace of the world?

____ 3. Do you frequently do two or more things at once?

____ 4. Do you often become involved in several projects at the same time?

____ 5. Does relaxing and doing absolutely nothing for several hours make you feel guilty?

____ 6. Do you become irritated out of proportion with others' slowness?

____ 7. Do you have a habit of looking at your watch or clock often?

____ 8. Do you emphasize strongly various key words in your speech, even when no real need for this exists?

____ 9. Do you hurry your sentences along, finishing the last few words as quickly as possible?

WEEK FOUR: MAKING STRESS WORK FOR YOU

_____ 10. Are you preoccupied with your own thoughts?

_____ 11. Are you preoccupied with acquiring material possessions?

_____ 12. Do you feel a chronic sense of having too little time?

_____ 13. Do you have any characteristic gestures or nervous tics?

_____ 14. Do you feel the need to handle every problem alone?

_____ 15. Do you feel that part of your success is due to your ability to do things faster than others?

_____ 16. Are you preoccupied with evaluating your performance and that of others in terms of productivity?

_____ 17. Do you have little time for hobbies or nonproductive (in terms of money) activities?

_____ 18. Are you referred to by others as being "hard-driving?"

_____ 19. When you meet another Type A personality, do you feel compassion for her affliction?

_____ 20. When you meet another Type A personality, do you feel the need to challenge her?

WEEK FOUR: MAKING STRESS WORK FOR YOU

What was your score on the SPPE in Week One?_____

What is your present score?_____

Many of you will find that your scores have decreased dramatically because of increased awareness that you now have regarding stress.

You have effectively modified your life patterns, for the time. Remember, if you showed little or no improvement in scores, continuing to follow the suggestions for managing stress learned in these past weeks will soon result in improvement. The coping techniques which you have learned along the way should be given continued attention. You now have the tools for conquering the damaging effects of stress. Use them.

Let's measure how effective you have been in eliminating the danger signs of stress. The Stress Personality Pattern Evaluation measured your life pattern and the manner in which it helps to foster a certain response to stress. The Pressure Points Checklist responded to earlier, measured the signs of excessive stress which are a part of your life.

Fill out the Pressure Points Checklist form below.

WEEK FOUR: MAKING STRESS WORK FOR YOU

PRESSURE POINTS CHECKLIST

Instructions: Read over each item on this list of characteristic responses of individuals under stress and place an X next to those signs which describe your stress response(s).

_____ 1. Pain in the neck or the lower back
_____ 2. Frequent need to urinate
_____ 3. Excessive perspiring
_____ 4. Insomnia
_____ 5. Desire to strike out at others
_____ 6. Inability to relax
_____ 7. Pounding of the heart
_____ 8. Feeling of blood rushing to your head
_____ 9. Inability to concentrate
_____ 10. Headaches which last more than an hour
_____ 11. Nervous laughter or giggling
_____ 12. Heavy smoking
_____ 13. Feeling of disorientation
_____ 14. Undefinable fears and anxiety
_____ 15. Dryness of the mouth and the throat
_____ 16. Lack of appetite
_____ 17. Compulsive eating
_____ 18. Diarrhea
_____ 19. Indigestion
_____ 20. Queasiness in the stomach

WEEK FOUR: MAKING STRESS WORK FOR YOU

___ 21. Vomiting
___ 22. Stuttering
___ 23. Nervous tics
___ 24. Uncontrollable urge to cry
___ 25. Emotional tenseness
___ 26. Increased smoking
___ 27. Increased intake of alcohol
___ 28. Increased use of prescription drugs
___ 29. Frequent accidents
___ 30. Nightmares
___ 31. Grinding of teeth
___ 32. Pre-menstrual tension
___ 33. Missed menstrual cycle
___ 34. Impulsive behavior
___ 35. Fatigue
___ 36. Trembling
___ 37. Frequent loss of temper
___ 38. Acting edgy and keyed up
___ 39. Vertigo
___ 40. Desire to avoid others
___ 41. Depression
___ 42. Tendency to be upset by unexpected sounds
___ 43. Anxiety based on no specific cause
___ 44. Skin irritation

What was your score in Week One? _____
What is your present score? _____
Do you see a substantial difference? _____

WEEK FOUR: MAKING STRESS WORK FOR YOU

If you have seen a substantial decrease in the number of pressure points checked off, then congratulations! The fewer the danger signs in your life, the healthier and happier you will be (and show yourself to be). Many of you will have been successful in eliminating some really dangerous signs of stress from your lives. Once you fully recognize what your stressors are, and give careful thought to dealing with them and even eliminating damaging stress, then you can begin to live a more healthy and happy life. Once you no longer experience the frequent need to urinate, the nervous perspiration, the diarrhea, indigestion, queasiness in the stomach, and vomiting, or the increase in body-harming crutches (drugs, smoking, alcohol), you'll surely find that you won't miss them.

For those of you whose score change is not dramatic, there is the rest of your life to eliminate those danger signs. But — start now! By applying what you have learned about stress and stress reactions in general, and your particular stressors and stress responses, you can successfully become master of your stress. This may be the last week of the program, but the effort of managing stress isn't over for any of you — no matter how great the change in your scores.

Your stress reactions were conditioned responses—habits. Bad habits. And we all know how difficult habits are to break—and to keep broken. It will be very easy for old and negative reactions to stress situations to slip back into your lives. That's why you should be aware of the "trigger situations" which spell danger to you. To assess the effect of various "trigger situations," place yourself in the following roles and assess the possible means of managing stress in each situation.

TRIGGER SITUATION EXERCISE 1

A woman who has completed a stress-reduction program feels that she now has complete control over stress.

Her investments took a dive the other day and she began to binge on alcohol, food and cigarettes. She says that this one-day binge was all right since it was her "controlled" way of coping with her stress.

1. What happened to her?

   _____

   _____

   _____

   _____

2. What did she do wrong?

_____
_____
_____
_____

3. How should she have handled the stress?

_____
_____
_____
_____

Ideas to consider for this Trigger:

1. The binges are dangerous.
2. She may be using even small dips in finances as excuses.
3. Temporary and immediate relaxation is needed rather than liquor or other negative crutches.
4. Refer to Coping Techniques and Preventive Techniques.

WEEK FOUR: MAKING STRESS WORK FOR YOU

TRIGGER SITUATION EXERCISE 2

Sally takes night classes at an area college. The number of reported assaults on women in the area is rather high and women are generally cautioned against going out alone at night.

Last night, Sally began to leave her car after arriving after dusk for a class. She saw a large figure leaning against a nearby car, in the direction that she had to pass. She began to feel nauseous and her stomach started to ache. She began to shiver all over and her heart pounded wildly.

Too fearful to leave her car, she quickly locked her door and waited five minutes. When the figure neither left nor moved in that time, she decided to leave the parking lot and drive home. She has vowed not to go back again.

1. What are her stressors?

   _____
   _____
   _____
   _____

2. What did she do wrong?

   _____
   _____

3. How could she have handled the stress?

_____

_____

_____

_____

Ideas to Consider for this Trigger:

1. Retreat may have been the wisest move.
2. Her stress reaction indicates more subtle and hidden stressors.
3. How does this affect her future?

TRIGGER SITUATION EXERCISE 3

Shana's teen-age son has just begun driving. As a single mother with a tight budget, she can only afford to have one car in the family. Her son, however, wants to borrow the car to go out socially, to shop, etc. In the past, the use of the car has been an issue between them which has since been solved. They have agreed that certain days and hours are

WEEK FOUR: MAKING STRESS WORK FOR YOU

allotted to Shana's son for use of the car—and no more.

Three days ago, Shana watched in amazement as her son pulled out a set of keys that he had had made. He simply took the car without asking and not at an agreed-upon time.

Shana fumed and threw glassware at the kitchen walls. Her face turned a bright red.

When her son returned, she screamed at him loudly and told him that he no longer could use her car. If he didn't like it, she said, he could move.

1. What happened to Shana?

   _____

   _____

   _____

2. What did she do wrong?

   _____

   _____

   _____

3. How could she have better handled her stress?

WEEK FOUR: MAKING STRESS WORK FOR YOU

_____
_____
_____
_____

4. Is there any way that she could prepare herself for similar stress incidents?

_____
_____
_____
_____

Ideas to consider for this Trigger:

1. Shana's reaction was excessive.
2. Discipline for both Shana and her son appears needed.
3. Reread Coping Techniques.

TRIGGER SITUATION EXERCISE 4

Tess must commute sixty miles daily to her job (one way). Much of her time commuting is spent in heavy traffic which gives her a nervous stomach, bad headache and grouchy personality. She says

WEEK FOUR: MAKING STRESS WORK FOR YOU

that this is just the way life is and the way she is.

The other day, she was caught in an accident and was unbearable to be around all day. She eventually had to leave work early because of physical symptoms of stress.

1. What happened to her?

   _____
   _____
   _____
   _____

2. What is she doing wrong?

   _____
   _____
   _____
   _____

3. How might she deal more effectively with her stressors?

   _____
   _____
   _____
   _____

WEEK FOUR: MAKING STRESS WORK FOR YOU

Ideas to consider for this Trigger:

1. Life can change — *we* can make it change.
2. Giving in to extreme stress will kill us.
3. Temporary relaxation was needed, and while waiting for the traffic to clear, she could have gone through a relaxation exercise.

In addition to considering various "trigger" situations which can affect our lives, allowing ourselves to consider re-patterning can be extremely valuable in sharpening coping skills.

REPATTERNING EXERCISE 1

Sheila works for a very ambitious boss. In her drive to the top, the boss constantly bombards Sheila with reports to be done, appointments to be kept on her behalf, and work which keeps Sheila long after five p.m.

Sheila values her job as a junior executive but also loves her family and despises the long hours.

She grinds her teeth, suffers from indigestion, and is often fatigued, irritable and ill.

1. What is happening to her?

_____

_____

WEEK FOUR: MAKING STRESS WORK FOR YOU

_____
_____

2. What is she doing wrong?

_____
_____
_____
_____

3. How can she cope with the situation?

_____
_____
_____
_____

Ideas to consider for repatterning:

1. What are her stressors?
2. What can she do to solve the problem?
3. Is this simply a problem of communication?
4. What means has she of better managing the stress?
5. Can she deal with the problem in a better way than suffering silently?
6. Is she, perhaps, encouraging the problem?

REPATTERNING EXERCISE 2

Dale is a successful real estate broker, and the mother of two children, eight and ten years old. While making deals and showing homes during the day, she worries constantly that she is failing as a mother. As a single parent, she works hard once she returns home to be both mommy and housekeeper for the evening.

She loves her children and her job. In addition, she is the sole support of her children and knows that she must succeed.

She is often fatigued, guilty, anxious, irritable and has a variety of physical stress symptoms.

1. What are the stressors in her life?

   _____
   _____
   _____
   _____

2. How can she cope with her varied roles?

   _____
   _____
   _____
   _____

WEEK FOUR: MAKING STRESS WORK FOR YOU

3. What changes, if any, need to be made in her life to ease the stress?

_____

_____

_____

_____

Ideas to consider for repatterning:

1. What are her stressors?
2. What can she do to sort out her life?
3. How would a reordering of priorities help?
4. What better means are there of handling her stress?
5. Is she exacerbating the problem?

REPATTERNING EXERCISE 3

Diane's eighty-three-year-old father can no longer live alone at home. The thought of confining him to a nursing home makes her guilty, so she and her husband have agreed to take her father into their home.

Diane and her husband both have full and flourishing careers, and a family to raise. In addition,

WEEK FOUR: MAKING STRESS WORK FOR YOU

she and her father never did get along.

The aspect of her father moving in has made Diane irritable and hard to talk to. She has started grinding her teeth and has become physically ill. In addition, she has been refusing to talk it out with her husband. She and her husband fight a lot and the home has become a battleground.

1. What are her stressors?

   _____

   _____

   _____

   _____

2. What is she doing wrong?

   _____

   _____

   _____

   _____

3. What must she do to alleviate her stress and still do her perceived duty to her father?

   _____

   _____

WEEK FOUR: MAKING STRESS WORK FOR YOU

_____

_____

Ideas to consider for repatterning:

1. Determine what her stressors really are.
2. What are the options?
3. Talking about her problems with her husband would help her to sort it out.
4. Priorities are important here.

REPATTERNING EXERCISE 4

Alice runs her own business. She is a free-lance writing and research consultant. Most of the time, no matter how carefully she budgets her time, she is rushing to finish projects.

Clients give her one deadline then call to create an earlier deadline. She meets their demands because she can't afford to turn away business.

She grinds her teeth, suffers from stomach pains, drinks too much coffee, can't sleep without a drink of liquor at night and then has trouble getting up in the morning.

1. What are her stressors?

WEEK FOUR: MAKING STRESS WORK FOR YOU

_____
_____
_____
_____

2. What is she doing wrong?

_____
_____
_____
_____

3. How can she deal more effectively with her stress?

_____
_____
_____
_____

Ideas to consider for repatterning:

1. Is the stress self-imposed?
2. What are the options to the present pattern?
3. Whose problem is it anyway?
4. How can the business be made more manageable?

WEEK FOUR: MAKING STRESS WORK FOR YOU

While this may seem hard to believe because of your own emotional involvement in a situation, each of your own personal stress situations can be approached in basically the same manner as the role-playing scenarios. You have learned, through this program, that a continuing stress situation does not have to keep going on. Instead, through re-patterning of your life, you can create a life which is more creative and productive — and less stress-filled.

In addition, you have found that there are specific coping techniques which can be used when unexpected stress situations occur. Further, you are now aware of your stressors and stress responses. There will continue to be stress situations to plague you. Use your new techniques for managing stress in dealing with your stressors.

You shouldn't become complacent about your ability to deal with stress. Instead, take your "stress pulse" occasionally and respond to the Periodic Stress Checklist, which follows, about once every two weeks.

PERIODIC STRESS CHECKLIST

_____ 1. Is my present pace of life comfortable for me?

WEEK FOUR: MAKING STRESS WORK FOR YOU

_____ 2. Am I trying to do too much?

_____ 3. Am I pressing beyond my stress threshold?

_____ 4. Am I doing things I want to do?

_____ 5. Am I attempting to please others and not myself?

_____ 6. Am I attending social functions out of obligation and not with an eye toward having fun?

_____ 7. Have activities in my life become burdensome?

_____ 8. Can some or all of the burdensome activities in my life be eliminated?

_____ 9. How well do I feel physically? Mentally?

_____ 10. Am I sleeping and eating well?

_____ 11. Is my body tense and "tight" a lot of the time?

_____ 12. Do I revert to negative coping behavior?

_____ 13. Am I short-tempered and irritable?

_____ 14. Do I feel out of control in several aspects of my life?

_____ 15. Do I need more hours in my day?

If, after going through the checklist, you find that old and bad stress responses are emerging once again, review the Mastering Stress Program and use your coping skills to put your life back on course. Once you have been liberated from negative stress and negative stress responses, don't become their slave ever again.

12. Some Further Words On Relaxing

There are many little rewards in life which we can give ourselves to offset the minor stressors which plague us and which often grow to be unmanageable. To maintain her sense of perspective, a woman doesn't have to carry around the preventive techniques list or the list of coping skills. Instead of worrying about what to do if stressors should strike and concerning yourself with being prepared, it would be better if you would just resolve to enjoy life.

Enjoying life is much easier to accomplish than it might appear. It doesn't require that we take lavish vacations yearly to get away from it all. It doesn't require that we have tons of money, or expensive playthings. Instead, enjoying life consists of noticing and appreciating the little pleasures which surround us — and which often don't cost a penny.

A primary ingredient in enjoying life is treating yourself well. Stop for a moment before you protest that you don't have time to do anything special for yourself. Think about the many ways in which we show kindness and courtesy to acquaintances, friends and even strangers. We may do this out of true regard for others — or just to have others like us. Whatever the reason, there usually exists time for others in lives that hold no time for themselves.

Does that sound selfish? Good. Think about that word selfish for a moment. Most of us avoid any semblance of appearing "selfish" in our actions. The term has as obscene a set of associations, in its own way, as any four-letter word which adolescents throw around in challenge to their parents. But what is the shame in being selfish? Self-ish. Concern with the self.

From infancy to adulthood, we are taught to share our crayons, our cookies, our pencils, our wealth, etc., with others who have less than we do and who are in need. This is admirable, and I am certainly not advocating that we hoard money and possessions in a Scroogelike manner. However, when we refuse to share, as children or as adults, we often find ourselves labelled "selfish." Few of us would admit to wanting to be selfish.

For women, the obsession with not appearing selfish may be even stronger than for men. Women are stereotypically viewed as nurturers, the healing figure to whom the hurt can turn. We are painted as the givers—not the receivers. It is for the mother/wife/sweetheart/female friend to provide the solace while the men and children of this world pour out their troubles.

Many women have broken free of this stereotype, but many more have not. In taking on such great wholesale responsibility for the feelings of the human population, women have put their own needs aside. To exhibit self-concern, a self-ish feeling, is anathema to us. In such behavior, we tend to ignore the needs of someone very important—ourself.

There are many ways in which you can be self-ish and show a little self-love in addition to all of the concern which you exhibit to others. Why not take a mini-vacation and get away from it all for a few hours? You don't have to fly off to Acapulco to relax, just schedule two or three hours to do something which you have been desiring to do. Have lunch alone at a simple or elegant restaurant. Have a manicure or massage. Take a bubble bath. Go browsing in an antique store, clothing boutique or craft fair.

Stop in at the florist and buy yourself an inexpensive bouquet to place on your table or dresser.

You can relax and take time off from stress by imagining a variety of rewards. Why not paint "daydream pictures?" Sit back in a comfortable chair, put up your feet and close your eyes. Conjure up pleasant memories or fantasies of every sort. It is your fantasy, so you can be as tranquil or sensual as you wish. What's your pleasure? Will the fantasy be childlike, Walter Mitty fare, sexual? The choice is yours.

Relaxation needn't be a solitary activity and we sometimes enjoy our leisure more when it is shared with others — our children, spouse, lover, family, friends. Visit a zoo or museum with a child and see it through a youngster's perspective. Visit the zoo or museum with your lover and enjoy the difference it makes to have someone you love sharing the experience. Have dinner by candlelight with someone else. That someone else needn't be a lover or spouse. You'll be surprised how relaxing dinner by candlelight can be when shared with a child, a parent, a friend.

Run through the snow. Jog in the early morning. Walk through crunchy leaves. Run in the rain.

Above all, whichever approach you take to relaxing and to leaving the stress behind, if only temporarily, enjoy your life. All women — wives, mothers, career women, housewives — need some "me time." You deserve to be selfish and, even more importantly, you *need* to be selfish to recharge.

Take a look around and see the little pleasures in life which help to keep us functioning smoothly from day to day. Recognize that stress can be offset by life's pleasures and enjoy life.